U0540019

Bodhi Light Tales

Volume ④

By Venerable Master Hsing Yun

星雲說喻 中英對照版

星雲大師 著

精進 On Diligence

Bodhi Light Tales: Volume 4 / 星雲說喻 中英對照版④
By Venerable Master Hsing Yun
星雲大師 著

Editor-in-Chief: Venerable Miao Guang
主編：妙光法師

Editorial and Translation Committee:
Fo Guang Shan Institute of Humanistic Buddhism, Center of International Affairs
英文編輯/翻譯：財團法人佛光山人間佛教研究院國際中心

Front Cover Illustrator: Venerable Youji
封面繪圖：有紀法師

Illustrators: Venerable Youji, Venerable Dao Pu, and Sedona
內頁繪圖：有紀法師、道璞法師、Sedona Garcia

Published and Distributed by: Gandha Samudra Culture Co. Ltd.
出版/發行：香海文化事業有限公司
Address: No.117, Section 3, Sanhe Road, Sanchong District, Taiwan R.O.C.
地址：241台灣新北市三重區三和路三段117號6樓
Tel 電話：+886-2-2971-6868
Fax 傳真：+886-2-2971-6577

Price 定價：NTD350（USD30）
Published 出版：May 2025/2025年5月
ISBN:978-626-98849-9-5
All rights reserved.

人間佛教叢書
星雲說喻 中英對照版④

出版‧發行‧編製 香海文化事業有限公司
發行人 慈容法師ǀ執行長 妙蘊法師ǀ編輯部 賴瀅如 蔡惠琪ǀ美術設計 許廣僑
香海悅讀網 https://gandhabooks.com ǀ 電子信箱 gandha@ecp.fgs.org.tw
劃撥帳號 19110467 ǀ 戶名 香海文化事業有限公司
登 記 證 局版北市業字第1107號

總 經 銷 時報文化出版企業股份有限公司
地址 333桃園縣龜山鄉萬壽路二段351號ǀ電話 (02)2306-6842

法律顧問 舒建中、毛英富ǀ版權所有 翻印必究
建議分類 寓言ǀ哲理

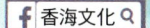

國家圖書館出版品預行編目(CIP)資料

星雲說喻4,Bodhi Light Tales Volume 4,
星雲大師(Venerable Master Hsing Yun)作.
-- 新北市 : 香海文化事業有限公司, 2025.05
168面 ; 27.9 X 21公分
中英對照版
ISBN 978-626-98849-9-5(精裝)

224.519   114003644

香海文化

香海悅讀網

Bodhi Light Tales
菩提心燈系列故事

Bodhi Light Tales
Volume ④

Biography of Venerable Master Hsing Yun 星雲大師簡介 6

Editor's Introduction 編者序 10

How to Use This Book 如何使用本書 14

Stories

01. The Four Wives 富翁與四位夫人 19
02. Where Is Happiness? 幸福在尾巴上 27
03. Tuning the String Properly 彈琴 35
04. The Third Floor 第三層樓 45
05. Steps of Life 人生的階梯 55
06. Persistence Is Key 伎兒得牛 67
07. The Poisonous Scorpion 毒蠍 77
08. To Have Only Stolen Once 偷自己的真心 87
09. The Bubble Necklace 水泡花鬘 95
10. The Lesson 就職第一課 105
11. Heavy Bag 還重嗎？ 117
12. Laziness Is Your Downfall 懶惰之害 127
13. A Mother's Love 背母親 139
14. The Squashed "Frog" 茄子喻 149
15. The Diligent Little Dog 小狗也會說話 157

Biography of Venerable Master Hsing Yun

Venerable Master Hsing Yun was born in 1927 in Jiangdu, Jiangsu Province, China. At the age of 12, he was tonsured by Venerable Master Zhikai in Qixia Temple, Nanjing, with Dajue Temple in Yixing, Jiangsu, as his ancestral temple. He later became the 48th-generation lineage holder of the Linji Chan school. In 1947, he graduated from Jiaoshan Buddhist College, and also trained at various Chan, Pure Land, and Vinaya monasteries, including Jinshan, Qixia, and others. He received a comprehensive Buddhist education in the lineage, teachings, and Vinaya disciplines. Later on, the Venerable Master was invited to serve as the principal of Baita Elementary School, and also the editor-in-chief of *Raging Billows Monthly*.

In the spring of 1949, the Venerable Master arrived in Taiwan. He served as the editor-in-chief of *Human Life Magazine*, *Buddhism Today Magazine*, and *Awakening the World*.

In 1967, the Venerable Master founded the Fo Guang Shan Buddhist Order, with the Four Objectives: to propagate the Dharma through culture; to foster talents through education; to benefit society through charity; to purify people's minds through spiritual cultivation. Guided by the principles of Humanistic Buddhism, he went on to establish over three hundred temples worldwide. Additionally, he oversaw the creation of various art galleries, libraries, publishing companies, bookstores, the *Merit Times* newspaper, and the Cloud and Water Mobile Clinic. Furthermore, he established sixteen Buddhist colleges and founded three high schools and five universities, including the University of the West in the United States, Fo Guang University in Taiwan, Nanhua University in Taiwan, Nan Tien Institute in Australia, and Guang Ming College in the Philippines. Notably, he also established the Institute of Humanistic Buddhism.

In 1970, the Venerable Master established Da Ci Children's Home and the Lanyang Ren Ai Senior Citizen's Home, providing shelter and care for vulnerable young children, and elderly individuals. He also actively engaged in emergency relief efforts, contributing to the fostering of a welfare society. Then, in 1991, he founded the Buddha's Light International Association (BLIA) and was elected as the President of the World Headquarters. Under his guidance, the association's mission expanded, symbolized by the saying, "the Buddha's Light shining over three thousand realms, and the Dharma water flowing continuously through the five continents."

In 1977, the *Fo Guang Buddhist Canon*, the *Fo Guang Dictionary of Buddhism*, and the 132-volume *Selected Chinese Buddhist Texts in Modern Language* were compiled. In 2017, the *Complete Works of Venerable Master Hsing Yun* was published, comprising 365 volumes with over 30 million words. In 2023, it was supplemented to 395 volumes, exceeding 40 million words, systematically expounding the ideologies, teachings, theories, and practical outcomes of Humanistic Buddhism.

In 2023, the Venerable Master peacefully passed away, his virtuous deeds complete and fulfilled, having reached the age of ninety-seven. He was revered as the Founding Master of the Fo Guang Order, and he left behind this poignant poem:

A mind with the compassionate vow to deliver sentient beings,

A body like a boat on the Dharma ocean, unbound.

Should you ask what I have achieved in this lifetime?

Peace and happiness shine upon the five continents.

星雲大師簡介

　　星雲大師，江蘇江都人，一九二七年生，十二歲禮志開上人為師，祖庭江蘇宜興大覺寺，傳臨濟正宗第四十八世。一九四七年於焦山佛學院畢業，期間曾參學金山、棲霞等禪淨律學諸大叢林，歷經宗下、教下、律下等完整的佛門教育。之後應聘為白塔國小校長，主編《怒濤》月刊。

　　一九四九年春來臺，主編《人生雜誌》、《今日佛教》、《覺世》等佛教刊物。

　　一九六七年創建佛光山，樹立「以文化弘揚佛法，以教育培養人才，以慈善福利社會，以共修淨化人心」四大弘法宗旨，以「人間佛教」為宗風，先後在世界各地創建三百餘所道場，創辦多所美術館、圖書館、出版社、書局、人間福報、雲水醫院，興辦佛教學院十六所，中學三所，及西來、南華、佛光、南天、光明五所大學，及人間佛教研究院。

　　一九七〇年後，相繼成立「大慈育幼院」、「仁愛之家」，收容撫育無依之幼童、老人及從事急難救濟等福利社會。一九九一年成立「國際佛光會」，被推為總會會長，實踐「佛光普照三千界，法水長流五大洲」的理想。

　　一九七七年編纂《佛光大藏經》、《佛光大辭典》及《中國佛教經典寶藏精選白話版》等。二〇一七年出版《星雲大師全集》，共三百六十五冊，三千餘萬字，二〇二三年增補為三百九十五冊，逾四千萬字，有系統地闡述人間佛教的思想、學說、理論，以及實踐結果。

　　二〇二三年，大師住世緣盡，淨業圓滿，享耆壽九十七，被奉為佛光堂上第一代開山祖師，留遺偈：「心懷度眾慈悲願，身似法海不繫舟，問我一生何所求，平安幸福照五洲」。

Editor's Introduction

Bodhi Light Tales is a captivating 6-volume collection of stories focused on the Six Paramitas, narrated by the revered Venerable Master Hsing Yun. Originally published in Chinese as *Xingyun shuoyu* (星雲說喻), these Buddhist Tales by Venerable Master Hsing Yun emerged from his enlightening talks and lectures on Humanistic Buddhism. In 2019, we took the initiative to adapt these stories into English as an ongoing audiobook series for the Bodhi Light Tales Anchor Podcast channel. However, our ultimate vision has always been to present them in a book format. As the original stories were concise and lacked additional details, the English adaptations were intentionally modified from the Chinese. In essence, the English tales are not direct translations of their original Chinese counterparts. To ensure that readers of all ages, faiths, beliefs, and cultures can connect with these stories, we employed several key approaches during the transition from Chinese to English, which we will elaborate on below.

To make the main characters more relatable, we added background information such as their names, occupations, and personalities. Thorough research was conducted to maintain historical and factual accuracy. We hope this additional information will help readers delve deeper into their favorite characters and even encourage further exploration.

Each tale concludes with a summary of its morals, providing readers with a clear understanding of the story's meaning and key lessons. These summaries highlight challenges people face in today's world and offer practical applications for daily life.

Additionally, we included Dharma Words from Venerable Master Hsing Yun at the end of each story, offering readers a final nugget of wisdom to take away. These quotes were carefully selected based on their relevance to the moral of each story. Venerable Master Hsing Yun originally shared these words of encouragement and advice based on his life experiences, aiming to inspire mindfulness and guide individuals in times of uncertainty.

Remember, Buddha-nature resides within all of us, regardless of whether we practice Buddhism or not. Both children and adults have the power to better themselves and positively impact the world around them. Our sincere hope is that these stories will inspire people of all ages, instilling in them a sense of inspiration, courage, and compassion. May this collection serve as a source of inspiration as you navigate through life's journey toward self-awakening!

編者序

《星雲說喻 中英對照版》，是一套引人入勝的六冊選集，收編了九十五篇由敬愛的星雲大師講說，以六度波羅蜜為主題的故事。這些故事最初收錄在《星雲說喻》，大師喜歡在演講中穿插生動有趣的故事，以傳遞人間佛教思想與實踐的精髓。

2019年，我們首次將《星雲說喻》的內容翻譯成英文有聲故事書，並於 Anchor 播客平台推出「菩提心燈」系列故事 (Bodhi Light Tales Podcast)。這些年，我們一直期待著將這些故事結集成冊，如今因緣條件具足，並以中英雙語圖書的形式呈現。為了讓來自各年齡層、宗教、信仰，以及文化的讀者皆能與故事產生共鳴，我們在精簡扼要的原文基礎上發揮想像，增添了一些原文故事沒有的情節。也就是說，這套故事書中的英文故事是經過編譯的創作，非中文的直譯對照。編譯的幾項原則要點說明如下：

首先是對故事人物的背景資訊加以補充，如：名字、所從事行業，及個性等。我們蒐集文獻和查證史料，以確保人物的歷史背景正確無誤。希望藉由建構鮮明的人物特性，能帶給讀者更多親和力，也鼓勵讀者進一步探索喜愛的角色。

第二，提綱挈領出每篇故事的主旨和寓意，讓讀者更容易把握住故事所要傳達的信息，引導省思。同時，也探討人們在現當代可能面臨的挑戰，幫助讀者連結所學，實際應用在日常生活之中。

故事結束，為每篇故事搭配一則精選「星雲法語」，作為總結故事核心寓意的智慧錦囊。「星雲法語」原是大師依據自己的人生經歷寫下的鼓勵和箴言，期望藉此帶給大家正念，在人生迷茫處作一盞指引方向的明燈。

學佛與否，佛性本自具足。無論是兒童還是成人，我們都有能力讓自己和周遭的世界變得更好、更正向。希望這套故事書能啟迪心性，讓各個年齡層的讀者在邁向自我覺醒的生命旅程中，充滿能量、勇氣和慈悲。

How to Use This Book

如何使用本書

Bodhi Light Tales by Venerable Master Hsing Yun are selected stories on the Six Paramitas: Generosity, Precept, Patience, Diligence, Meditative Concentration, and Wisdom. These short stories, in a 6-volume set, offer readers opportunities to contemplate the Buddha's teachings and concepts of Humanistic Buddhism.

星雲大師著《星雲說喻 中英對照版》收錄以六度波羅蜜為主題的精選故事：布施、持戒、忍辱、精進、禪定、般若。此系列共有6冊，讓讀者有機會透過故事思維佛陀的教義和人間佛教的理念。

Title Page 篇章頁

1. Category
one of the Six Paramitas

類別 六度波羅蜜之一

2. Story Title
in English and Chinese

中英文故事篇名

3. QR Code to Audio
a. Scan the QR code
b. Scroll down to find story title
c. Press ▶ to listen

掃碼聽故事
a. 掃描二維碼
b. 點選故事
c. ▶ 播放與聆聽故事

01

On Diligence
The Four Wives
富翁與四位夫人

Bodhi Light Tales
1 The Four Wives

Story Pages 故事內容

4. Illustration
繪圖

5. Story (in English)
English adaptation
英文故事

6. Story (in Chinese)
Original content, as told by Venerable Master Hsing Yun
中文故事

7. Vocabulary List
English keywords with Chinese definitions to guide bilingual readers

詞彙表
英文關鍵詞彙及其中文解釋，
為雙語讀者提供輔助閱讀資源。

Once upon a time, there was a rich old man who knew he would soon pass away. He thought, "Since I cannot take my wealth with me, why don't I find someone to go with me to the next life?"

This rich old man had four wives. He called out to his fourth wife, whom he loved most dearly, "You're the one I love most. I've bought you lots of pearls[1] and diamonds. When I die, will you come with me?"

Upon hearing this, the fourth wife replied, "I am very grateful[2] that you've loved me dearly. But when you die, that will be the end of our life together. I don't want to go with you!"

The rich old man then thought of his third wife. All along she had been well treated[3] and he had never abandoned[4] her. After hearing her husband's request[5], the third wife replied, "I'm still young and I can remarry, so why don't you have some compassion for me and find someone else?"

The old man then turned to his second

VOCABULARY
1. pearls (n.) 珍珠
2. grateful (adj.) 感激的
3. treated (v.) 對待
4. abandoned (v.) 拋棄；離棄
5. request (n.) 請求

從前，有一位富翁年紀老邁，不久就要離開世間。他心想：萬貫的家財帶不走，不如找個人來陪我，這樣黃泉路上也有個伴。

富翁有四個太太，最疼愛的年輕貌美的四太，他將她喚來：「平常我繼愛妳，送妳很多珍珠、鑽戒，現在我不久於人世，妳就陪我一起走吧。」四太太一聽，花容失色地表示：「生前愛我，我很感謝，但你死了就死了，我們夫妻一場，只是一段因緣，我可不想跟你一起走。」

- 21 -

- 16 -

8. Dharma Words

Quote from Venerable Master Hsing Yun expressing the heart of each story

星雲大師法語
總結故事的核心價值和寓意

Dharma Words by Venerable Master Hsing Yun

The real treasure of energy is not
in the mountains or in the oceans,
but in one's own mind;
The real treasure of the Dharma is not
in the sutras or in the mouth,
but in one's own mind.

星雲大師法語

真正的能源寶藏，
不在山裡，不在海裡，
在於自己的心裡；
真正的佛法寶藏，
不在經裡，不在口裡，
在於自己的心裡。

01

On Diligence

The Four Wives

富翁與四位夫人

Bodhi Light Tales
1 The Four Wives

Mind

Relatives & Friends

Wealth

Body

Scan me to listen!
掃我，聆聽故事！

Once upon a time, there was a rich old man who knew he would soon pass away. He thought, "Since I cannot take my wealth with me, why don't I find someone to go with me to the next life?"

This rich old man had four wives. He called out to his fourth wife, whom he loved most dearly, "You're the one I love most. I've bought you lots of pearls[1] and diamonds. When I die, will you come with me?"

Upon hearing this, the fourth wife replied, "I am very grateful[2] that you've loved me dearly. But when you die, that will be the end of our life together. I don't want to go with you!"

The rich old man then thought of his third wife. All along she had been well treated[3] and he had never abandoned[4] her. After hearing her husband's request[5], the third wife replied, "I'm still young and I can remarry, so why don't you have some compassion for me and find someone else?"

The old man then turned to his second

VOCABULARY

1. pearls (n.) 珍珠
2. grateful (adj.) 感激的
3. treated (v.) 對待
4. abandoned (v.) 拋棄；離棄
5. request (n.) 請求

　　從前，有一位富翁年紀老邁，不久就要離開世間。他心想：萬貫的家財帶不走，不如找個人來陪我，這樣黃泉路上也有個伴。

　　富翁有四個太太，最疼愛的年輕貌美的四太太，他將她喚來：「平常我最愛妳，送妳最多珍珠、鑽戒，現在我不久於人世，妳就陪我一起走吧。」四太太一聽，花容失色地表示：「生前愛我，我很感謝，但你死了就死了，我們夫妻一場，只是一段因緣，我可不想跟你一起走。」

wife, who answered, "I can't possibly go with you, I am taking care of everything in this house! Don't worry, after you die, I'll make sure you have a good funeral. Since you're my husband, I promise[6] to personally take your body to the crematorium[7]."

Having been rejected[8] by his three wives, he was left with his first wife whom he had long neglected[9] and for whom he had never bought anything. "She probably wouldn't say yes," he thought. Still, he was afraid to die alone and he gathered the courage[10] to ask his first wife, "I'm leaving this world soon, will you come with me?" Unexpectedly, the first wife said, "We're husband and wife, we're meant to be together. Wherever you go, I'll go, when you die, of course, I'll come with you!"

VOCABULARY

6. promise (v.) 答應
7. crematorium (n.) 火葬場
8. rejected (v.) 拒絕
9. neglected (v.) 忽視；疏忽
10. courage (n.) 勇氣

於是富翁找來三太太，告訴她自己平時待她不薄，不曾離棄過她，如今要她陪葬。但三太太聽完富翁的請求，驚慌不已：「我還年輕，你死了，我可以改嫁，你就發發慈悲，找其他人吧！」富翁只得再找二太太。二太太說：「我沒有辦法陪你一起死，家裡大小的事都是我在打點，甚至你死了以後，我要替你張羅喪葬事宜。念在夫妻的情分上，我會親自送你到墳場。」

The moral of this story is that we each have four wives. The beloved fourth wife represents our body. We often forget to care for its health. We wear accessories[11] to make it look beautiful, but after we die, our bodies cannot come with us.

The third wife represents[12] our wealth. We often try to protect[13] it because we're so afraid[14] of losing our money, but sadly, when we die, we cannot take any of it with us.

The second wife represents our relatives and friends. Every once in a while, we give them some love and care, but after we die, all they can do for us is perhaps send us off to the crematorium, and then return to their own busy lives.

What does the first wife represent? She is our mind, which we usually fail[15] to take care of until we meet with death. Only our mind follows us

VOCABULARY

11. accessories (n.) 飾品
12. represents (v.) 代表
13. protect (v.) 保護
14. afraid (adj.) 害怕的；擔憂的
15. fail (v.) 未做；未履行

富翁被三個太太一一回絕，心裡很傷心，不得已去找大老婆。但富翁自知平日對她也沒有半句關心，也從來沒有買什麼禮物送她，我這麼冷落她，她可能不會答應。富翁實在害怕一個人孤零零地走，最後還是鼓起勇氣，小聲地問：「我不久於人世，妳願意陪我一起走嗎？」不料大老婆即刻回答說：「夫妻本是同林鳥，嫁雞隨雞，嫁狗隨狗，你死了我當然跟你一起走。」

everywhere, however, because we are so lost in our desires, our mind tends to follow evil and delusive[16] paths, drifting[17] about aimlessly[18].

So please care for your body and keep it healthy. Enjoy your possessions[19] and the joy they offer. Cherish your friends and family, for the love that they provide. But most importantly, look after your mind and nurture[20] goodness in it by spending some time on your own, taking time to read, take time to chant, or to meditate. Because it is your most faithful companion that will take your merits and the results of your deeds into your future lives.

四個太太的故事，隱喻的是我們人的一生。最鍾愛的四太太就是我們的身體，我們無時無刻不關心它的健康，讓它穿金戴玉，打扮光鮮，但是人死了，身體是不能跟我們一起走；三太太，就是我們積聚的財產，平時悉心保護它，害怕被別人占有，只可惜在我們面臨死亡時，它也不會跟隨我們；二太太，代表的是我們的親戚朋友，偶爾往來，也給他們一些小惠，到了我們死的時候，他們也許來上個香，送我們一程，然後就各自要忙著生計。而大老婆是什麼？就是我們這顆心，平時最不關心它，但是直到生命的盡頭，這顆心卻與我們生死相隨，只是我們陷入五欲貪愛中，隨妄心惡念，四處飄搖流浪。

人縱然得到全世界的財富，仍找不到自己的真心，就像富翁活著時，糊里糊塗；死時，迷惑恐懼。色身、財富、妻妾一樣也帶不走，只有善業惡業跟隨我們，往來天堂地獄。

VOCABULARY

16. delusive (adj.) 錯誤的；虛假的
17. drifting (v.) 漂流
18. aimlessly (adv.) 漫無目的地
19. possessions (n.) 擁有；財產
20. nurture (v.) 培養

Dharma Words by Venerable Master Hsing Yun

The real treasure of energy is not
in the mountains or in the oceans,
but in one's own mind;
The real treasure of the Dharma is not
in the sutras or in the mouth,
but in one's own mind.

星雲大師法語

真正的能源寶藏,
不在山裡,不在海裡,
在於自己的心裡;
真正的佛法寶藏,
不在經裡,不在口裡,
在於自己的心裡。

02

On Diligence

Where Is Happiness?

幸福在尾巴上

Bodhi Light Tales
2 Where Is Happiness

Scan me to listen!
掃我,聆聽故事!

Once upon a time, there were two homeless dogs who had only each other. Sport, the younger dog, often complained about being poor. He wondered when the god of happiness would finally rid[1] them of the shame of being deprived[2] and homeless. He dreamed of someone, anyone providing them with food and shelter[3].

Doc, the older dog, seeking to comfort Sport, said, "Being homeless means that our home is everywhere and anywhere. Don't be greedy, be content with any food and warmth you can find. You would lose your dignity[4] and your freedom if you had to beg a master for such favors."

But Sport refused to listen to his elder's advice. He continued to have grand dreams about being a pedigree[5] dog, cared for and

有二條狗，彼此相依為命。小狗老是抱怨生活的窮困，幸福之神不知道何年何月才會降臨，使牠們衣食無虞，以洗刷「喪家之犬」的羞辱。老狗總是安慰小狗：「無家處處是家，生活只要溫飽就足夠了，被人類豢養，要做一隻搖尾乞憐的狗，反而失去尊嚴和自由。」

小狗，聽不進老狗的意見，一心作著「流浪狗變名貴狗」的美夢。

VOCABULARY

1. rid (v.) 擺脫
2. deprived (adj.) 匱乏的；貧寒的
3. shelter (n.) 庇護所
4. dignity (n.) 尊嚴
5. pedigree (adj.) 純種系譜的

cherished.

One day, he decided to visit a fortune teller. "Where is Happiness?" he asked.

The fortune-teller pointed and replied, "Happiness is on your tail."

Upon hearing this, Sport began to chase[6] his own tail. In circles and circles he kept going, until dejected[7] and covered in sweat, he gave up when he realized it was impossible to catch his own tail.

Feeling miserable[8], he found Doc and told him, "The fortune-teller told me that happiness was on my tail, but try as I might, I couldn't catch it. Do you know how I might catch happiness?"

Doc laughed and replied, "I find happiness by never regretting[9] the past, never fearing the present, and never worrying about the future. I always march[10] forward, knowing happiness on my tail will follow me wherever I go."

VOCABULARY

6. chase (v.) 追逐
7. dejected (adj.) 沮喪的；灰心的
8. miserable (adj.) 痛苦的
9. regretting (v.) 遺憾；後悔
10. march (v.) 行走；前進

有一天，小狗跑去算命占卜，牠問：「幸福到底在哪裡？」

「幸福就在你的尾巴上。」小狗聽完，為了要抓住幸福，拚命轉著圈子，要咬住自己的尾巴。

小狗跑得滿身大汗，還是咬不到自己的尾巴，垂頭喪氣地對老狗說：「占卜說，我的幸福在尾巴上，可是我卻抓不住幸福，老狗，你有什麼辦法可以抓得住幸福呢？」

So where is happiness?

Happiness follows when we are content with what we have in life.

Happiness follows when we show appreciation[11] to those who have helped and supported[12] us in times of need.

Happiness follows when we trust that there is hope in our future, so long as we choose to never look back and keep marching forward.

So there is no need to chase happiness, so long as we have the causes for happiness, it will follow us everywhere we go.

VOCABULARY

11. appreciation (n.) 感激
12. supported (v.) 幫助;支持

老狗笑說:「我尋找幸福是向前走,對過去無悔,對現在無懼,對未來無憂。因此只要我的腳步向前,尾巴上的幸福快樂自然就跟隨我。」

幸福在哪裡?猜忌使我們遠離幸福的目光,懷疑使我們錯過幸福的召喚,嫉妒使我們模糊幸福的面貌,妄想使我們失去幸福的擁抱。

何必向神祇乞求幸福的降臨,要佛祖喜捨幸福的地圖?幸福,原本就在我們的心靈。

Dharma Words by Venerable Master Hsing Yun

Avoid suffering to gain happiness.
Realize impermanence to gain hope.
Realize non-self to gain friendship.
Understand emptiness to gain from emptiness.
Avoid bad karma to gain a better life.

星雲大師法語

要遠離「苦聚」，才能獲得安樂。
要知道「無常」，才能擁有希望。
要懂得「無我」，才能融入大眾。
要明白「空性」，才能真空妙有。
要消除「惡業」，才能美善人生。

notes

03

On Diligence

Tuning the String Properly

彈琴

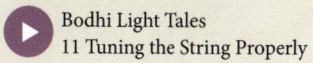

Scan me to listen!
掃我，聆聽故事!

Once upon a time, there was a novice monk who took his Buddhist practices very seriously. He was very dedicated[1] and diligent[2].

Each morning, he would wake up before the sound of the morning bell. With everyone still asleep, he would sit and meditate. During recess[3], when everyone was resting, he kept working.

He told himself, "The Buddha teaches us that a clean environment reflects[4] a clean mind. So I must do my very best to keep the monastery clean."

On some nights, the novice monk would not even sleep. Instead, he practiced his walking meditation. Eventually, due to exhaustion[5] and a lack of rest, he fainted while cleaning the meditation hall and was brought back to his room.

When the novice monk woke up and realized what had happened, he cried, "The path in front of me seems so very long but I'm so very tired. I really want to practice, but

VOCABULARY

1. dedicated (adj.) 盡心盡力的；盡職盡責的
2. diligent (adj.) 勤勉的；用功的
3. recess (n.) 休息
4. reflects (v.) 反射；反映
5. exhaustion (n.) 疲憊；筋疲力盡

　　佛陀在世時，出家弟子中有一位修行十分精進勇猛的比丘，名叫聞二百億耳，由於他太過精進勇猛，在日夜刻苦的修持下，身體逐漸疲憊，雖到了難以支撐的地步，仍開不了悟，心中非常煩惱，因此，就向佛陀請求還俗。

I don't think I have the energy to keep going."

He felt that the only way out was to quit[6] and as a result, he was very ashamed[7]. Heartbroken and weeping[8], he went to say goodbye to his Teacher.

"Teacher, I request[9] your permission[10] to leave. I am unable to continue on this path. As I have no energy left."

The Teacher looked at him kindly, and asked, "What was your profession before becoming a monk?"

He replied, "Teacher, before becoming a monk, I was a musician. I played the guitar."

With a kind and understanding voice, the Teacher continued, "If you tune the string on your guitar too tightly, what will happen when you start to play?"

"The string will break," said the novice monk.

"If the string is tuned too loosely, what will happen?" the Teacher asked again.

"If the string is too loose, it will not make a

VOCABULARY

6. quit (v.) 放棄
7. ashamed (adj.) 慚愧的
8. weeping (v.) 哭泣
9. request (v.) 請求
10. permission (n.) 准許；允許

「佛陀！出家修行太辛苦了，我要回到世俗去！」

佛陀慈悲端詳眼前這位弟子，看來既疲倦又沮喪，問道：

「你過去是做什麼的？」

「我是彈琴的音樂家。」

sound. Nothing could be played," answered the novice monk.

The Teacher smiled at him. "There you have it. The path of practice is like tuning a string on a guitar. If we practice too intensely[11], the string is too tight. And it will snap[12] easily and so will we. However, if we are lazy, and let the days slip by[13] without improving ourselves, then the string is too loose and won't play. We will have wasted this precious human life."

The Teacher continued, "As you are, if you leave the monastery, you will continue to work yourself to exhaustion. True practice is to find a balance[14] between diligence and rest, suffering and joy, pain and pleasure. True practice is to walk the Middle Path between the two extremes[15]. Do you understand?"

VOCABULARY

11. intensely (adv.) 激烈地
12. snap (v.) 拉斷
13. slip by (p.v.) 流逝
14. balance (n.) 平衡
15. extremes (n.) 極端

「我問你：假如琴的絃很緊，彈的結果會怎麼樣呢？」

「絃太緊會斷。」

「如果太鬆呢？」

「太鬆則琴不響。」

The novice monk had a moment of awakening[16]. He smiled, "I understand now. Practicing is just like tuning a string. We cannot be too tight. And we cannot be too loose. We need to find just the right balance in order to play beautiful music!"

Deciding to stay, from that day on, the novice monk made great progress in his practice. He finally understood what it means to practice the Middle Path[17].

The moral of the story tells us that the path of self-improvement[18] and the path of spiritual practice is a lifelong journey.

Just as Venerable Master Hsing Yun says, "Step back to jump further. Crouch back to spring higher.

Rest to walk longer. Withdraw to learn better.

In your lifelong journey, press forward, but relax when things bog[19] you down.

In your lifelong journey, be steadfast[20], but stay

VOCABULARY

16. awakening (n.) 覺醒
17. Middle Path (n.) 中道
18. self-improvement (n.) 自我改善
19. bog (v.) 陷於泥淖
20. steadfast (adj.) 堅定不移的

佛陀微笑地說：「聞二百億耳，修行也和彈琴一樣，太過勇猛精進，就像太緊的琴絃容易斷；太懈怠不認真，就像太鬆的琴絃彈不響，所以修行的生活要中道。你常常苦行，苦行太苦了，就會感到修行冷冰冰的，沒有意思。你若回到俗家去，太過快樂反而容易樂極忘形。因此，真正的修道生活，要不苦也不樂，行之中道，這才是真正的修行。」

calm when you feel overwhelmed[21]."

We need to cultivate[22] wisdom to find the right balance for ourselves.

So, work, when it is time to work.

Rest, when it is time to rest.

Practice, when it is time to practice.

Play, when it is time to play.

Remember, cultivating mindfulness[23] means to walk the Middle Path without falling into either extremes, just as practicing is like tuning a string.

VOCABULARY

21. overwhelmed (v.) 受打擊
22. cultivate (v.) 培養
23. mindfulness (n.) 正念

修行太緊太鬆，是許多修行人都容易犯的過失。有的人太過著急，用苦行壓迫自己，使身心如繃緊的弦，反而不能灑脫自在；反之，有的人懈怠、放逸，空度時日，終不能開悟證道。

在超凡入聖的修行路上，是不能偏於一邊的，唯有不急不緩、不苦不樂、不忙不閒，把身心安住在中道的生活裡，維護自己在一個平衡調和的位置，才能增進道業，逐漸解脫證悟。

Dharma Words by Venerable Master Hsing Yun

Step back to jump further.
Crouch back to spring higher.
Rest to walk longer.
Withdraw to learn better.

星雲大師法語

退後,是為了跳得更遠。
壓縮,是為了彈得更高。
休息,是為了走得更長。
韜光,是為了學得更博。

notes

04

On Diligence

The Third Floor

第三層樓

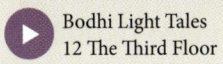

Scan me to listen!
掃我，聆聽故事!

Once upon a time, a merchant named Marcus went abroad on a business trip. Over there, he was invited by his friend, James, to his house to have dinner.

"Welcome to my house, my dear friend. It is great to see you again after so long," said James.

"James, it is great to see you too! You have such a beautiful house," admired[1] Marcus.

"Let me show you around my house," offered James happily.

Marcus quickly saw that James paid great attention[2] to every detail[3], as everything in the house was made of the finest materials. Everything was just perfect.

When they reached the third floor of the house, Marcus was even more impressed[4] by the amazing view from the balcony. It was the most beautiful scenery he had ever seen in his whole life.

The view was like something out of a movie. He saw an entire valley of lush green fields, all glowing[5] in the light of the setting sun. Far out

VOCABULARY

1. admired (v.) 欽佩；愛慕
2. attention (n.) 關注
3. detail (n.) 細節
4. impressed (v.) 使印象深刻
5. glowing (v.) 發光

久遠以前，有一個大富翁很希望自己能擁有一棟三層樓的房子，於是遣人找來了一位建築師。建築師一到，大富翁就問：「你可不可以幫我建造一棟三層樓高的房子？」建築師聽後，當下應允，並且說：「依照目前的技術，建築三層樓的房子是沒有問題的。」

in the distance, the mountains were tall and majestic[6]. A pack of birds flew by, singing their beautiful songs.

"How amazing[7]! This view is simply fantastic[8]! I have never seen anything like this. I am going to build a third floor and a balcony too when I get back," exclaimed[9] Marcus.

As he made his way back to his own home, Marcus kept thinking about the view he saw and dreamt of what he would see once his third floor and balcony were finally built.

He planned to have a nice cup of hot coffee up there every morning after breakfast. After every hard day of work, he would look at the beautiful sunset every evening. On weekends, he could invite his friends to his house for dinner and they would all enjoy the view together.

Marcus could not stop thinking about how happy he would be once he had his "third floor."

When he arrived home, Marcus immediately[10] hired a team of builders to construct his "third floor."

VOCABULARY

6. majestic (adj.) 宏偉的
7. amazing (adj.) 驚人的；令人驚喜的
8. fantastic (adj.) 極好的
9. exclaimed (v.) 驚叫
10. immediately (adv.) 立即；馬上

　　不過，就在建築師即將開始打地基的時候，大富翁卻對他說：「一般人都好笨啊，建房子總是從第一層建起，我可不要這麼傻，浪費建第一層、第二層的錢幹什麼？你只要幫我建第三層就好了。」

"As quick as you can please! Build me the third floor with a beautiful view!" demanded[11] Marcus.

The team drew up a building plan. Then, as they started work by laying the foundation[12], they were stopped by Marcus.

"What are you doing?" he asked the builders.

"Didn't you want us to build a three-story mansion[13]?" they asked.

"Yes, but I just want the third floor," said Marcus impatiently[14]. "I don't want a first or second floor."

"That is impossible, sir. The third floor can only be built on a good foundation, meaning a first and second floor. You cannot build the third floor by itself!" explained the workers.

However, Marcus insisted on wanting only the third floor without the necessary[15] foundations.

VOCABULARY

11. demanded (v.) 強烈要求
12. foundation (n.) 地基
13. mansion (n.) 大廈
14. impatiently (adv.) 無耐性地
15. necessary (adj.) 必需的；不可或缺的

建築師一聽，很為驚訝，就說：「哪有這種事？沒有第一層樓、第二層樓，怎麼會有第三層樓呢？」但是無論他怎麼說明，大富翁都認為太浪費，堅持只要第三層樓就好。

Eventually, fed up with this nonsense[16], the workers left, and Marcus did not have any house built, not to mention, his most desired[17] "third floor."

This story teaches us that only when we start from the ground up, and build a firm foundation upon the first and second floor, can we then enjoy a beautiful view from the third.

There is a saying, "Mighty oaks[18] from little acorns[19] grow." This means that great things come from small beginnings.

Just as Venerable Master Hsing Yun teaches, "The key to success is persistence[20].

The key to success is awareness of causes and conditions.

Strive for your goal, but don't be impatient.

There is no success except through hard work.

Success comes when you learn from your failures.

Just as a delicious food needs seasoning, results require practice and effort.

Modesty brings harmony;

Diligence brings achievement.

VOCABULARY

16. nonsense (n.) 胡扯；胡鬧
17. desired (adj.) 想要的；渴望獲得的
18. oaks (n.) 橡樹
19. acorns (n.) 橡子
20. persistence (n.) 堅持不懈

這一則《百喻經》的譬喻故事，正說明了世間上很多人不重視基礎，只幻想著能夠一步登天，都只是空中樓閣罷了。尤其在這個追求速度的時代，凡事都求速成，生病了，要吃特效藥；吃飯了，或者來一碗速食麵；連熱菜，也多使用微波爐，一、二分鐘就能燙熱。然而事實上，我們應該要知道，速成的東西就像許多廉價的物品一樣，是不能耐久的。

Kindness and patience reveal your grace."

Whether in our worldly lives, or our spiritual[21] cultivation[22], it is essential to first establish[23] a strong foundation with great care.

Only with a strong foundation will results take care of themselves.

In this way, we will have a beautiful "third floor" in our lives, from which we can enjoy the wonderful view of our achievements.

VOCABULARY

21. spiritual (adj.) 精神上的
22. cultivation (n.) 培養;修行
23. establish (v.) 創建;建立

所謂「萬丈高樓平地起」,想成就什麼事情,必須一步一腳印,逐漸累積,才能成其高、成其大、成其長遠;相對的,基礎不穩固的高、大,那必然是不能持久的。

Dharma Words by Venerable Master Hsing Yun

Strive for your goal, but don't be impatient.
There is no success except through hard work.
Success comes when you learn from your failures.

星雲大師法語

爭氣，不要生氣。
成功要靠自己努力，別無他途。
失敗要靠自己檢討，猶有可為。

notes

05

On Diligence

Steps of Life

人生的階梯

Bodhi Light Tales
77 Steps of Life

Scan me to listen!
掃我，聆聽故事!

Once upon a time, there lived two brothers, Mark and Jayden. As entrepreneurs[1], they invested in a hotel downtown, using the penthouses[2] on the eightieth floor as their homes. Mark and Jayden enjoyed hiking[3] and recently decided to take on the Pacific Crest Trail hiking challenge, which spans 2,650 miles from Mexico to the United States and ending up in Canada. So, they began to train every weekend to prepare themselves physically as well as mentally.

One day, they had just returned from training. When they got to the elevator, there was a sign that said, "The elevators are currently out of order. We apologize for the inconvenience[4]."

Jayden sighed and said, "You must be kidding[5]…"

"Are you up for a challenge?" Mark asked.

"Are you thinking what I'm thinking?" Jayden replied.

Mark nodded and began running towards

VOCABULARY

1. entrepreneurs (n.) 企業家
2. penthouses (n.) 頂層公寓；頂層客房
3. hiking (n.) 遠足；健行
4. inconvenience (n.) 不便
5. kidding (v.) 開玩笑

　　有兄弟兩人外出登山，下山後準備回到八十層樓的家，正好碰上大樓的電梯故障。兩兄弟自許為登山好手，何懼八十層高樓，於是振奮起精神，往上爬行。

the stairs.

　　Jayden yelled, "Wait for me!" and then ran after his brother.

　　Since they had been training, they ran up to the twentieth floor with ease[6]. However, when they reached the fortieth floor, their legs began to shake. Their heavy backpacks[7], filled with all their equipment, were weighing them down. Feeling tired, they sat on the stairs.

　　Jayden whined[8], "Seems like it was a bad idea to take on this challenge."

　　"It's not that bad," Mark replied.

　　"My legs hurt, and my backpack is too heavy!" Jayden exclaimed[9].

　　"Imagine us in the middle of the Pacific Crest Trail, what would we do then? This is why we're training. Come on! Don't give up so easily. Always think positive," Mark replied.

　　"Don't lecture[10] me! You keep going if you want! I'm going to sit here for a bit," Jayden said.

　　"Okay, taking time to rest is also important

VOCABULARY

6. ease (n.) 容易；不費力
7. backpacks (n.) 背包
8. whined (v.) 抱怨
9. exclaimed (v.) 大聲說
10. lecture (v.) 教訓

　　爬到二十層樓，兩人仍不覺疲累氣喘，繼續努力向上爬。到四十層樓時，兩人開始感到腿酸，背在身上的行李裝載著登山器具更顯沉重，於是決定暫時放在第四十層樓，等到有電梯可乘時，再來取回。

when hiking. If we need to rest, then let's rest, but let's not give up," Mark replied. He fished in his backpack for some snacks. Finding some cheese crackers, he offered them to Jayden.

Now feeling slightly[11] better, Jayden came up with an idea, he suggested, "I know! Let's leave our backpacks here, and come pick them up when the elevators are working again. What do you think?"

"I'm going to continue with my backpack. If I was doing the challenge[12], I couldn't just leave my backpack behind. So, I'm keeping mine on my back," Mark replied.

Jayden shrugged[13] and said, "All right fine! I'm leaving mine here."

Without his heavy backpack, Jayden ran up the stairs, soon leaving Mark behind. Struggling[14] to keep up with Jayden, huffing and puffing[15], Mark yelled, "Let's take another rest here."

When they both looked up, they realized they were on the sixtieth floor.

VOCABULARY

11. slightly (adv.) 稍微
12. challenge (n.) 挑戰
13. shrugged (v.) 聳肩
14. struggling (v.) 掙扎
15. huffing and puffing (v.) 喘大氣

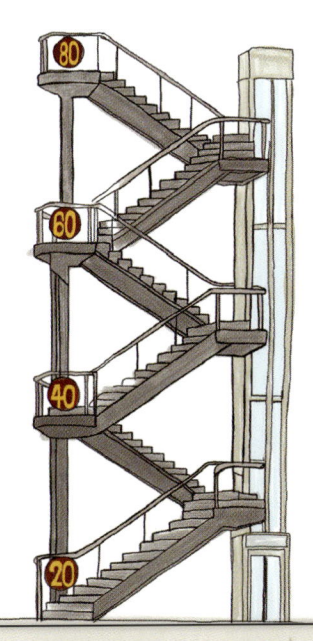

"See! You should have listened to me on the fortieth floor and left your backpack," Jayden said smugly[16].

Mark sat down on the stairs and began sipping[17] his water. It was then Jayden realized that he did not have his water with him. Mark smiled and said, "Want some?" Jayden nodded.

Resting his head on his knees, Jayden looked at Mark and said, "Can I ask you a question?"

"You just did, so go ahead!" replied Mark.

"Why did you and Julia divorce[18]? It seemed you were going to be together forever. What happened?" Jayden asked.

Mark sighed and said, "Sometimes, we don't realize how important someone is until we lose[19] them. I didn't realize how little time I spent with her. I guess she felt I loved my career more than her because I was working 24/7. It was my fault[20] for not being

VOCABULARY

16. smugly (adv.) 得意地
17. sipping (v.) 啜飲
18. divorce (v.) 離婚
19. lose (v.) 失去
20. fault (n.) 過錯；過失

到了六十層，已經感覺吃力，氣喘噓噓，無力再往上爬，又想只剩下二十層，還有何難？最後的二十層階梯，儘管辛苦、疲倦、氣喘、流汗、力盡，他們還是

there for her. I thought I needed to provide her a comfortable life by focusing on my career, but all she wanted was for me to spend time with her. I was selfish and couldn't see things from her perspective[21]."

"I see. Would you do things differently if you had another chance?" Jayden asked.

"Definitely! I would consider the pros[22] and cons[23] carefully. Honestly, I was too immature[24] back then when we got married," Mark replied.

"I'm sure you'll meet someone again," Jayden said.

"Thanks. Shall we continue with the remaining twenty floors?" Mark replied.

"Sure! We can't give up now, we've made it this far!" Jayden said as he stood, ready to go.

Up the last twenty floors, they really struggled, tired and out of breath, but they persisted[25]. When they finally reached the eightieth floor, they were completely exhausted.

Catching his breath, Jayden exclaimed, "Finally! We're home!" He rushed to the door

VOCABULARY

21. perspective (n.) 觀點;想法
22. pros (n.) 優點
23. cons (n.) 缺點
24. immature (adj.) 不成熟的
25. persisted (v.) 堅持

堅持爬到第八十層樓。當哥哥準備要開門時,忽然大喊:「糟糕!鎖匙放在行李中,沒有帶上來!」兄弟兩人頓時如洩氣的皮球一般,感到一片茫然!

of his penthouse, rummaging[26] around for his keys, and then he screamed, "Oh no! My keys, they're in my backpack!"

At that moment, Mark smugly waved his keys and opened the door to his penthouse. Realizing he had not weighed the pros and cons when he left his backpack on the fortieth floor, Jayden, now alone in the corridor[27], fell to the floor like a deflated[28] balloon.

This story illustrates the span of one's lifetime. The eighty floors represent a life of eighty years. The first twenty floors depict[29] our youth. When we are young and full of energy, we're quick on our feet, willing to innovate[30] and be fast learners. We see the world with fresh eyes full of wonder and yearn for adventure. We're a force of nature in human form ready to go full-out.

As we reach forty years old, or the fortieth floor, life is now more focused on the important choices we make. This period is considered to be the peak of one's career, where we are working our hardest to realize our dreams, making ends meet, and dealing with important life-changing decisions. The heavy backpacks in this

VOCABULARY

26. rummaging (v.) 到處翻尋
27. corridor (n.) 走廊
28. deflated (adj.) 縮小的；洩氣的
29. depict (v.) 描述
30. innovate (v.) 改革；創新

八十層階梯意喻人生八十年歲月，年輕力壯時，思考活躍、學習力強，盡天下事物都是試得冒險與嘗試的新鮮物。四十歲以後的人生，正值事業頂峰，叱吒風雲於職場，或為實踐理想，或為糊口生活，卯足全力奮

story represent all the things that potentially[31] weigh us down, whether it be career, marriage, family, or health.

As we now reach the sixtieth floor, aged sixty, our physical strength is in decline[32]. Having experienced all the joys and sorrows[33] of life, we see life differently. Some only now begin to live life with enjoyment and contentment[34].

Finally, when we reach the eightieth floor, aged eighty, we discover that our body is old. Our teeth are no longer as white or strong, our hair is gray and white, and we feel rather fragile[35].

In this story, Jayden decided to let go of his backpack that was filled with everything important to him. However, when we seek to open the various doors throughout our lives, we find that the key to our happiness was in that "heavy backpack" we left behind. Each of us carries different things in our backpacks. It may be our aging parents, our healthy body, our happy family, our travels, and so on. As we age, and climb up the stairs of our lives, to reduce the weight of our "heavy backpack," we may put down our perceived

VOCABULARY

31. potentially (adv.) 可能地；潛在地
32. decline (n.) 衰弱；衰退
33. sorrows (n.) 悲傷
34. contentment (n.) 滿足；知足
35. fragile (adj.) 脆弱的；虛弱的

鬥。六十歲以後，體力已大不如前，閱盡人間喜怒哀樂事，開始為享受而生活。到了八十歲，齒已搖，髮已蒼白，終究要開啟生命的大門，卻發現幸福的鑰匙還放在「沉重的行李」中，忘了拿。

burdens[36] one at a time. However, when we are old and fragile, looking back, we realize that we no longer have the strength to bring back true happiness. Therefore, it is important to consider carefully when making decisions, so that we can seize[37] each opportunity[38] that comes our way.

VOCABULARY

36. burdens (n.) 負擔
37. seize (v.) 把握
38. opportunity (n.) 時機；機會

沉重的行李，人人認知不同。可能是高堂老父母，可能是健康身體，還有美滿家庭、旅遊參學，往上爬行時為了減輕重量，我們一一擱下，卻待老來回首過往，空嘆真正的幸福已無力回頭取了。

Dharma Words by Venerable Master Hsing Yun

Everything has its pros and cons;
simply understand how to weigh them.
Always keep sight of what is possible,
for even dry stone and rotten wood can be used as medicine.

星雲大師法語

凡事皆有利弊,只要懂得權衡之道,
往大處著眼,枯石朽木也能入藥。

06

On Diligence

Persistence Is Key

伎兒得牛

Bodhi Light Tales
98 Persistence Is Key

Scan me to listen!
掃我，聆聽故事！

Once upon a time, there lived a young musician in a village named Sid. He earned a living as a street performer[1]. Sid's musical talent was well-known and appreciated[2] by all.

One day, Sid was performing and the whole town enjoyed his beautiful music. A passerby went up to Sid, handed him a flyer, and said, "They're holding a music contest[3], maybe you should give it a go."

Sid read the flyer[4], and when he saw the reward for winning the contest was a cow, he thought to himself, "If I win a cow, my family will have a good source of income. Besides, I've nothing to lose." So, Sid signed up for the contest.

When Sid arrived at the contest venue, he was ushered[5] into a hall with the other contestants. The host then announced, "Welcome to Olav's Music Contest. We are honored to have so many talented musicians here today. Before we begin, let us explain the rules. Each contestant will have a maximum of

VOCABULARY

1. performer (n.) 表演者
2. appreciated (v.) 欣賞
3. contest (n.) 競賽
4. flyer (n.) 傳單
5. ushered (v.) 引導

有一名擅長各式各樣樂技的伎兒，演奏的技巧出神入化，曲曲都能扣人心弦。他的才藝過人，備受眾人肯定。

ten minutes to play their favorite piece of music. The judges will assess each contestant's tone, technique[6], rhythm[7], and stage presence. And now... let us begin..."

One by one, each contestant went on stage to perform their best piece of music. The competition was fierce as the judges carefully considered each performance. When it was time to reveal[8] the winner, the judges announced, "Today's contest featured performances of the highest level. It was difficult to decide an overall winner, so we have a tie, the winners are Sid and Jules."

As Sid and Jules made their way to the stage to receive the prize, the organizer, Olav, quickly called the emcee[9] over and said, "The prize is one cow only, I cannot share one cow between two winners. I don't want to lose face in front of everyone and be criticized[10]. So, to decide the ultimate winner

VOCABULARY

6. technique (n.) 技巧；技術
7. rhythm (n.) 節奏；韻律
8. reveal (v.) 透露；揭露
9. emcee (n.) 司儀；節目主持人
10. criticized (v.) 批評

一次，這個伎兒到一戶富貴人家乞牛。性格慳吝的富人，不願意施捨牛隻，又怕遭人非議，被人批評為富不仁，因此故意出了一道難題：「要我給你一頭牛可以，不過我有一個條件，你必須為我日夜不停地演奏，持續演奏一年，自然可以得到你應有的報酬。」

between them, set the following challenge: they must each play their music nonstop for a whole year in my palace. Whoever gives up first, loses. Whoever wins gets the cow as the prize."

After the challenge was announced[11] to both winners, Sid spoke up, "Sure, but I have a question. Are you sure you won't get tired of hearing the same music nonstop for a whole year?"

Olav confidently[12] replied, "Maybe you'll give up before I get tired of listening! Let's see who can play their music nonstop. You shall play, and I shall listen!"

"It's a deal[13]!" Sid said.

The following morning, Sid and Jules arrived at the palace and began playing their music.

The day after, Jules almost gave up[14], but on seeing Sid's enthusiasm[15], pushed himself to continue.

On the morning of the third day, however, Jules gave up and left. Sid, on the other hand,

VOCABULARY

11. announced (v.) 宣布
12. confidently (adv.) 信心十足地
13. deal (n.) 交易
14. gave up (p.v.) 放棄
15. enthusiasm (n.) 熱情；熱誠

這個伎兒爽快地回答：「這沒問題，但是您果真能持續聽上一年不厭倦嗎？」

富人自信滿滿地說：「你能演奏，我就能聽。」

still enjoyed playing his music. By noon, Olav began to feel sick and tired of listening to the same music over and over again. So, he tried to discourage[16] Sid by telling him, "Jules gave up, aren't you going to give up as well?"

"No! The deal was that I'd play my music for a whole year. It hasn't even been three days yet. A deal is a deal, I'm not giving up," Sid replied while continuing to play his music.

By the end of the week, Olav was now extremely annoyed[17] and couldn't bear[18] to listen anymore. He signaled his attendant to bring the prize cow, and said to Sid, "I want you to stop playing right now. Here is your reward. Please just stop playing."

Confused, Sid asked, "It hasn't been a year yet. Are you sure you want me to stop?"

"Yes," Olav replied as the cow was brought in. He continued, "I admire your perseverance[19]. Please take the cow, you've won it fair and square[20]."

Feeling extremely happy, Sid said, "Ok,

VOCABULARY

16. discourage (v.) 勸阻
17. annoyed (adj.) 煩惱的；惱怒的
18. bear (v.) 忍受；容忍
19. perseverance (n.) 毅力
20. fair and square (phrase) 正大光明的；公平公正的

於是，伎兒窮日落月，一心一意不停地演奏。才不過三天的時光，富人已經越聽越不耐煩，看伎兒還專注陶醉地演奏，趕緊命令僕人牽一頭牛給伎兒，急匆匆地打發他離開。

thank you very much." Sid packed his instrument and left the palace with his cow.

This story highlights the importance of perseverance and the willpower[21] to succeed. Sid achieved his goal and was rewarded because he never thought about quitting[22]. Even as Olav tried to discourage him, Sid kept his promise and continued to play his music.

The Buddha taught us that diligence is the path to liberation. Diligence is the key to opening the door to success. It is like drilling[23] a piece of wood to make fire. If you do not keep at it long enough, no sparks will appear and no fire will be produced. Similarly, to be truly liberated[24], continuous cultivation is required. Such is the function of diligence.

In practicing Buddhism, one must diligently continue to learn and deepen their understanding of the core teachings. If we want to acquire[25] knowledge, learn various skills, and be successful,

VOCABULARY

21. willpower (n.) 意志力
22. quitting (n.) 放棄；退出
23. drilling (v.) 鑽孔
24. liberated (adj.) 解脫的
25. acquire (v.) 取得；學到

佛陀強調，精進是通向解脫彼岸的不二法門。在修學佛法的過程中，要能深入法要，離繫解脫，必須靠自己不斷努力行持，這就是精進力的功用。

we must practice diligence and perseverance. The same is true for Buddhist practitioners. With diligence, we will progress[26]. Eventually, we will be able to fulfill our ideals[27] and accomplish[28] our goals.

VOCABULARY

26. progress (v.) 進步;改進
27. ideals (n.) 理想
28. accomplish (v.) 完成;實現

　　精進是開啟成功之門的鑰匙,精進就像是鑽木取火,持續不間斷才會生出火苗。譬喻故事裡的伎兒,因為有恆心毅力與堅持,所以能達成他的目標而得到牛。在世間也一樣:求取知識學問,學習各項技能,想要有成就,就得靠一份精進心、恆常力;修學佛法者也是,一旦有精進力驅動,自然日有所進,而圓滿菩提道。

Dharma Words by Venerable Master Hsing Yun

With only five minutes of enthusiasm, you shall fail.
To persevere even through the last five minutes, you shall succeed.

星雲大師法語

失敗者,往往是熱度只有五分鐘的人;
成功者,往往是堅持最後五分鐘的人。

07

On Diligence

The Poisonous Scorpion

毒蠍

Bodhi Light Tales
37 The Poisonous Scorpion

Scan me to listen!
掃我，聆聽故事!

Once upon a time, there lived a poisonous scorpion on the riverbank[1]. As days, weeks, and months passed, he thought to himself, "I'm so tired of this boring[2] life, it feels like I've been living here forever! A change of scenery[3] would be nice. I wonder what's on the other side of the river…"

Since then, the scorpion could only think about how he could cross the river. Then another thought came to him, maybe if one of the animals around here would consent[4] to help him cross! Little did he know, all the animals were scared of him.

One morning, as the scorpion wandered[5] around the riverbank, he heard the kangaroo yell to the possum, "Quick! Run! The scorpion is here!" Before the scorpion could even say anything, they were gone. Even the koala, sitting high in the tree, kept a watchful eye on the scorpion, and warned the other animals, "Go! Hurry!! He's getting closer to you!" They would all stay as far away from the scorpion to avoid

VOCABULARY

1. riverbank (n.) 河岸
2. boring (adj.) 無聊的
3. scenery (n.) 風景；景色
4. consent (v.) 同意
5. wandered (v.) 漫步；徘徊

佛經裡記載：有一隻毒蠍住在河的右岸一段時間，牠靜極思動，想換個不同的環境。由於毒蠍身上的劇毒，其他的動物無不畏懼萬分，即使毒蠍再三承諾，絕對不會用毒刺傷害牠們，但是空中的鳥，水裡的魚，都拒絕毒蠍渡河的乞求，深怕自己生命會不保。

any chance of being stung[6] and poisoned.

Utterly disappointed, the scorpion knew that getting help to cross the river was going to be a challenge. However, he did not wish to give up. He went around asking for help and tried very hard to convince[7] all the animals that he would not sting them, but no one was willing to take the risk. The birds in the sky and the fish in the river all rejected the scorpion's request for help crossing the river. All were scared their lives would be in danger.

Each day, the scorpion would look at the other shore, sad that he did not have wings to fly across. He also admired[8] the fish, who had the freedom to swim leisurely[9] in the river.

One day, the sky was clear and the sun was shining. Again, the scorpion went for a stroll[10] along his riverbank. He then saw a turtle slowly making his way towards him.

VOCABULARY

6. stung (v.) 刺
7. convince (v.) 使信服
8. admired (v.) 羨慕
9. leisurely (adv.) 悠閒地
10. stroll (n.) 漫步

每天，毒蠍望著潺潺的河水興歎，恨自己身上沒有長翅膀，無法飛越兩岸；更羨慕魚兒來去的悠游自在。有一天，天氣晴朗，毒蠍在河岸上散步，看到遠地來的一隻烏龜。毒蠍上前向烏龜拜託：「烏龜先生，我想學習您四處旅行參學的偉大精神，我要到河的另一邊去旅行，請您載我一程。」

Without hesitation[11], the scorpion said, "Turtle, I would like to be like you, always learning and seeking new adventures, roaming[12] around. I would like to travel to the other side of the river. Can you please take me over there?"

The turtle answered reluctantly[13], "I'm willing to help you, but your poisonous sting could kill me. How can I trust you?"

The scorpion beat his own chest and replied, "I promise you I won't! Besides, you are carrying me across the river. My life is in your hands. If I was to poison you, how would that benefit me? Why would I do something so silly[14]? Please help me, you are my only hope."

Seeing the scorpion pleading[15], the turtle said, "All right, but remember your promise not to sting me, okay?"

"Yes, yes! I promise!" The scorpion replied happily. He then hopped onto the turtle's back.

The turtle swam hard and fast across the river. But, on the verge of reaching the other side, he felt a sharp sting on the back of his

VOCABULARY

11. hesitation (n.) 猶豫
12. roaming (v.) 閒逛
13. reluctantly (adv.) 不情願地
14. silly (adj.) 愚蠢的；傻的
15. pleading (v.) 懇求

烏龜聽了以後，面有難色地回答：「我是樂意幫忙，但是你身上的毒刺會使人致命，我怎能相信一隻毒蠍的話呢？」

毒蠍拍拍胸脯說：「烏龜先生，你載負我渡河，你我就是生命的共同體，我如果用毒刺傷你，對我自己也不利，我怎麼會做出損人又不利己的傻事呢？」

head. Angry, the turtle yelled at the scorpion, "You ungrateful scorpion! You stung me with your poison on purpose! I knew you could not be trusted! Now, we are both going to drown and die… Why would you even do such a thing?"

Feeling guilty and regretful, the scorpion replied, "I didn't mean to hurt you. Please forgive me. I am really sorry for what happened. I have been a scorpion for so long that it is in my nature to sting and use my poison. I really didn't mean to do it."

This story highlights that we all have our own habits. If we develop habits of love and compassion, our minds will remain pure and we will be at ease. If we develop the habits of cherishing[16] and building affinities[17] with others, it can lead us to good affinities. However, developing bad habits such as greed and jealousy is like trapping[18] our minds in the locked gates of hell. We will constantly be stranded[19] in a sea of suffering.

The Buddha said, "Life is impermanent, just like the morning dew." Water drops are fleeting[20],

VOCABULARY

16. cherishing (v.) 珍愛；愛護
17. affinities (n.) 緣
18. trapping (v.) 困住
19. stranded (v.) 被困住
20. fleeting (v.) 稍縱即逝

烏龜最後答應壽蠍的請求，讓牠坐在背上。當烏龜賣力地往前游去，就在即將抵達彼岸時，烏龜的頭被刺了一下，烏龜生氣地罵壽蠍：「你這隻忘恩負義的壽蠍，你用毒刺刺我，我們都會同歸於盡，你為什麼要做出違背良心的事？」

壽蠍無限委屈地回答：「烏龜先生，請你原諒我，我真的對不起你，但我做一隻壽蠍實在太久了，不知不覺中，我就會拔出身上的刺……」

nothing lasts forever. Despite the savings that we may deposit in our bank accounts, there's no guarantee we will always make an income from it. Life is short. So, we should learn to practice loving-kindness, doing kind deeds, and being the master of our own lives.

We should practice discipline[21], meditative concentration[22], and wisdom[23] to subdue[24] the poisonous scorpion in our minds. We should remove the poisonous sting from ourselves in order to safely arrive on the other side of the river.

VOCABULARY

21. discipline (n.) 戒；紀律
22. meditative concentration (n.) 定
23. wisdom (n.) 慧
24. subdue (v.) 制服；控制

　　人常常有各種習慣，倘若有慈悲柔和的習慣，則可以讓我們身心清涼自在；有惜福結緣的習慣，可以使我們得到許多增上善緣。如果染上不好的惡習，如貪瞋嫉妒的等等煩惱習氣，則會使我們羈鎖在黑暗地獄裡，漂流在生死苦海中。

　　佛陀也常說：人命無常，喻如朝露，出息雖存，入息難保。在如此短促的人生，當多多熏習清淨莊嚴的善行，能夠做得了自己的主人，用戒、定、慧降伏心裡的毒蠍，拔除身上的毒刺，才能安全的渡到彼岸。

Dharma Words by Venerable Master Hsing Yun

Repeated action becomes a habit.
Habit becomes a character.
A character becomes fate.
Fate rules your life.

星雲大師法語

重複的舉止,會變成習慣。
定型的習慣,會變成個性。
個性的所向,會決定命運。
命運的好壞,會決定一生。

notes

08

On Diligence

To Have Only Stolen Once

偷自己的真心

Bodhi Light Tales
6 To Have Only Stolen Once

Scan me to listen!
掃我,聆聽故事!

Once upon a time, Chan Master Shiwu left the temple to travel.

On his way, he met Peter, a fellow[1] traveler. They started to chat and both realized they got along quite well. As night fell, they decided to share a room at a hotel nearby.

In the middle of the night, Master Shiwu heard noises inside the room.

"Is it morning already?" the Master asked.

"No, it's still nighttime," replied Peter.

So Master Shiwu tried to fall back to sleep, yet Peter kept making noises. All of a sudden[2], the Master felt him approaching[3] his bed. Startled[4], the Master woke up and caught Peter by the arm.

"What are you doing? Who are you?" said the Master.

Peter realized he had been caught red-handed[5], and saw no point in lying.

"I'm sorry, Master. I am a thief."

Master Shiwu nodded and asked, "So, how long have you been a thief?"

VOCABULARY

1. fellow (adj.) 同伴的
2. all of a sudden (phrase) 突然
3. approaching (v.) 靠近
4. startled (v.) 使大吃一驚；使嚇一跳
5. red-handed (adj.) 現行犯的

石屋禪師外出，碰到一位陌生人，暢談之下，不覺天色已晚，兩人因此投宿旅店。半夜，石屋禪師聽到房內有聲音，就問：「天亮了嗎？」對方回答：「沒有，現在仍是深夜。」石屋心想，此人能在深夜漆黑中起床摸索，一定是見道很高的人，或許還是個羅漢吧？於是又問：「你到底是誰？」

「是小偷！」

石屋：「哦！原來是個小偷，你前後偷過幾次？」

Peter sat down and confessed[6], "I have been a thief for quite some time now. I'm not really sure how many times I've stolen things or even when I began to steal."

The Master sat down as well and continued his inquiry[7], "What makes you happy about stealing? Why do you keep stealing? Does it not keep you happy for long?

Peter replied, "It depends on how and what I steal and its value. The longest I've been happy after stealing was a week. After that, I felt unhappy and felt the need to steal again."

Master Shiwu laughed and said, "So, you're a small-time crook[8] who steals only small things. Haven't you considered maybe stealing something bigger?"

Dumbstruck[9], Peter asked, "Have you stolen something Master? It sounds like you speak from experience."

Master Shiwu replied immediately, "I have, but I have only stolen once!"

Even more astonished[10], Peter pressed on,

VOCABULARY

6. confessed (v.) 承認
7. inquiry (n.) 詢問
8. crook (n.) 罪犯
9. dumbstruck (adj.) 嚇得發憷的
10. astonished (adj.) 驚異的

小偷：「數不清。」

石屋：「每偷一次，能快樂多久呢？」

小偷：「那要看偷的東西，其價值如何！」

石屋：「最快樂時能維持多久？」

小偷：「幾天而已，過後仍不快樂。」

石屋：「原來是個鼠賊，為什麼不大大的做一次呢？」

小偷：「你有經驗嗎？你共偷過幾次？」

石屋：「只一次。」

"Once? Only once? How is that possible? Why had you only stolen once?"

The Master answered, "I've only stolen once. But, I am able to enjoy what I stole my whole life, even right now."

Stunned[11], Peter pleaded[12], "Please Master, tell me what you did and how you did it!"

Master Shiwu suddenly grabbed[13] Peter and pointed a finger at his heart. "It was this. Do you understand? This is a boundless[14] treasure, right here. If you spend your whole life committed[15] to this, you will lack for nothing in your life. Happiness will always be within your reach."

Peter replied, "A part of me understands, but another part doesn't."

The Master smiled and said, "All in good time. All in good time, Peter."

Moved by the Master's words, Peter asked to become his student so that he could learn from his wisdom.

VOCABULARY

11. stunned (adj.) 目瞪口呆的
12. pleaded (v.) 乞求；懇求
13. grabbed (v.) 抓握
14. boundless (adj.) 無限的
15. committed (v.) 致力於；投入

小偷：「只一次？這樣『夠』嗎？」

石屋：「雖只一次，但畢生受用不盡。」

小偷：「這東西是在哪裡偷的？能教我嗎？」

石屋禪師一聽，一把抓住鼠賊的衣襟，指著他的胸口說：「這個你懂嗎？這是無窮無盡的寶藏，你將一生真正奉獻在此事業上，畢生受用不盡，你懂嗎？」

小偷：「好像懂，又好像不懂，不過這種感受卻是我未曾有過的。」

The moral of this story is, why are we always so focused[16] on material things found outside ourselves? Why do we often forget the treasures that exist in our own minds? The treasures within us are more valuable than anything found on Earth. True happiness comes from understanding our minds. By cultivating[17] our minds through listening to the Buddha's teachings, contemplating[18] them, and putting them into practice, we will be able to transform and transcend[19] birth and death. The treasure within your mind is infinite[20] and yours to keep.

VOCABULARY

16. focused (adj.) 聚焦的
17. cultivating (v.) 培養；修行
18. contemplating (v.) 沉思
19. transcend (v.) 超越
20. infinite (adj.) 無限的

我們總是看到心外的財富，沒有發現心中無窮盡的財富；總放著這些取之不竭用之不盡的寶藏，去竊取外在有形的寶藏。聰明的人兒，何不用心將自心的慈悲、忍耐、智慧偷到手，成為一個真正富有的人！

Dharma Words by Venerable Master Hsing Yun

No money, no opportunity—let it be,
cultivate merit and wisdom to reach nirvana.
Little clothing, little food—let it be,
seek treasure in your mind.

星雲大師法語

無錢無緣由他去,只修福慧作慈航;
少衣少食不計較,只求心內有寶藏。

09

On Diligence

The Bubble Necklace

水泡花鬘

Bodhi Light Tales
8 The Bubble Necklace

Scan me to listen!
掃我，聆聽故事!

Once upon a time, there lived a King named Louis who loved his little Princess Bella so much, he would give her anything she wished for.

On one rainy afternoon, the little Princess looked at a pond outside her window. She noticed[1] that as raindrops[2] fell into the pond, cute little bubbles were formed[3].

"Look at those pretty bubbles! I must have them!" said Princess Bella.

So she ran to the king and demanded[4], "Father! I want a necklace made of those bubbles."

"What do you mean, my dear?" King Louis asked gently.

"I saw some pretty bubbles on the lily pond. I want a necklace made of those bubbles now," demanded Princess Bella.

King Louis shook his head and said, "I don't think it's possible, my dear. Those bubbles are too fragile[5]..."

"No!" cried Princess Bella. "I want it now! Make it happen! Please... Father."

VOCABULARY

1. noticed (v.) 注意到
2. raindrops (n.) 雨滴
3. formed (v.) 形成
4. demanded (v.) 要求
5. fragile (adj.) 脆弱的；易破的

有一個國王老年得女，真是視若掌上明珠，百般的疼愛。這位小公主美麗非常，也喜歡向國王撒嬌，不時提出許多無理的要求，而國王都毫不猶豫地滿足小公主的願望。

一場小雨下過，在花園裡遊玩的小公主無意間看到池面的水泡映著天光，閃著眩人的光彩，她被水泡的華美給迷惑了。於是向國王表示，身上的真珠項鍊不比水泡花鬘漂亮，要求國王給她一條水泡製成的花鬘。

King Louis couldn't bear to see his Princess cry. So he gathered[6] all the florists in his kingdom at the pond.

"Make me a necklace out of these bubbles," he demanded.

The florists all looked worried[7].

"But my King, that is impossible," said one of them. "Bubbles burst[8] at the slightest[9] touch! How are we able to make a bubble necklace?"

Although King Louis knew he was right. He just couldn't bear to see his Princess cry.

"No one leaves this palace alive without a bubble necklace!" said the King. So everyone fell silent[10]. And some even cried because they knew it was just impossible.

Suddenly, a voice spoke up softly, "Let me try, my King." It was Old Anthony, the oldest florist in the Kingdom. "I can make a bubble necklace."

"If you can, I will

VOCABULARY

6. gathered (v.) 聚集
7. worried (adj.) 擔心的；憂慮的
8. burst (v.) 爆裂；破裂
9. slightest (adj.) 最輕微的
10. silent (adj.) 沉默的

世間哪有水泡花鬘呢？可是無論國王怎麼向公主說明，公主仍執意要得到水泡花鬘，還大發脾氣，說：「如果找不到美麗的水泡花鬘，我就永遠不吃飯。」

國王明知小公主驕蠻無理，但是一想到絕食的小公主性命恐怕不保，心裡著急得不得了，只好召來全國的工匠、藝術家，希望他們幫忙想個辦法，撈起水泡，串成一條花鬘。所有的工匠、藝術家一致搖頭，異口同聲的說：「水泡怎麼可能做成花鬘呢？」

spare[11] you all," said King Louis.

"However, I have one request," continued Anthony, "I will need help from the Princess to complete this task." So, the King brought Princess Bella to the pond.

"Dear Princess," said Anthony, "there are so many pretty[12] bubbles in the pond. Some are colorful, some are clear, some are big, and some are small. Which ones do you like? Please bring me the bubbles you like, so I can make a necklace out of them for you?"

"Sure!" Princess Bella agreed.

"I like this big one!" she said, and tried to lift[13] it out of the water. But as soon as she touched the bubble, it would burst. So she tried again with a smaller bubble, which also burst. No matter how gentle Princess Bella was, all the bubbles would burst upon touch.

Frustrated[14], Princess Bella pouted[15] her lips and said, "Fine! I don't want a bubble necklace anymore."

She then pointed at the flowers next to the

VOCABULARY

11. spare (v.) 饒恕
12. pretty (adj.) 漂亮的
13. lift (v.) 舉起
14. frustrated (adj.) 灰心的；氣餒的
15. pouted (v.) 撅嘴

「簡直是天方夜譚。」大家你一言我一語，直說不可能。其中，有個老工匠站出來說：「尊敬的國王！我有辦法把水泡做成花鬘。」

國王滿心期待地找來小公主，小公主眼睛發亮，問：「老公公，您真的能替我做一串水泡花鬘？」

老工匠微笑回答：「現在我們一起到水池邊，去做一條美麗的花鬘。」

pond, and demanded, "Just make me a flower necklace instead."

As the Princess stomped[16] back to the palace, King Louis, Old Anthony, and the florists all smiled at each other, feeling relieved[17].

The moral of the story is that we are all like the Princess. We try to grab[18] onto things that we think are real, but will never last.

Blinded by delusion[19] and desire, Princess Bella is attached to the pretty bubbles, thinking that her bubble necklace will make her happy. But how can something that is not real become our true happiness? We need to ask ourselves.

Just as said in the *Diamond Sutra*,

"All conditioned phenomena

Are like dreams, illusions, bubbles, shadows;

They are like drops of water and flashes of lightning.

Such is how everything in this world should be contemplated[20]."

The wise mind sees the illusion of things and knows that they are subject to constant change, just

VOCABULARY

16. stomped (v.) 跺；怒氣衝衝地走
17. relieved (v.) 鬆了口氣
18. grab (v.) 抓住；攫取
19. delusion (n.) 迷惑；錯覺
20. contemplated (v.) 沉思

皇宮的花園水池旁，擠滿了朝中的大臣們與上萬的工匠，每個人都在忖測，要看看這個老工匠到底在玩什麼把戲！

老工匠對小公主說：「公主，水面的泡泡很美，但是我不知道公主喜歡的花鬘是什麼式樣？請公主把水泡撈起來給我，我來串成花鬘。」小公主捉著水裡的泡泡，任憑她怎麼緊抓，水泡還是從她的指縫裡消失。當夕陽的餘暉照在水面時，小公主終於有所體悟，知曉水上泡沫是捉撈不住的。

like the setting sun and fleeting[21] clouds. Therefore, the wise mind remains unattached[22] to gain and loss and is willing to let go.

That is why Venerable Master Hsing Yun tells us,

"Wake up from your ignorance and realize the essence[23] of life.

Stop searching outside for your happiness but find the true treasures within.

Whoever subdues[24] anger, greed, and delusion will have inner joy.

Whoever realizes the true nature of impermanence can be free from suffering."

This is how we can face all gains and losses in life with the wisdom of the Buddha.

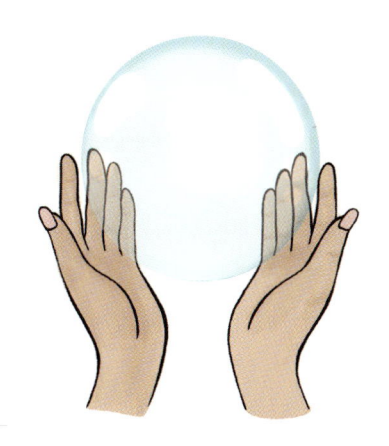

VOCABULARY

21. fleeting (adj.) 飛逝的；短暫的
22. unattached (adj.) 不執著的
23. essence (n.) 本質
24. subdues (v.) 制伏；控制

小公主寧可捨命，苦苦地追逐夢幻泡影，思惟吾人的生生世世又何嘗比故事中的小公主聰明幾分？誠如法眼文益禪師告誡世人的詩：「豔冶隨朝露，馨香逐晚風，何須待零落，然後始知空？」當徹知世間有為的無常虛妄，收拾起多年的身心狼藉，才能見到內心原有一塘碧水連天的無限遼闊。

誰縛了你？是我們迷於眼耳六根夢幻的假相，李白醉裡撈月，我們不也是經常如此嗎？只要令我們戀著，身心不得自由，都是一場水泡花鬘的逐雲追夢。

Dharma Words by Venerable Master Hsing Yun

Wake up from your ignorance and realize the essence of life.
Stop searching outside for your happiness but find the true treasures within.

星雲大師法語

人,要從愚癡迷夢中覺醒,才能認識生命的真諦。
人,要從向外貪求中回頭,才能找到內心的寶藏。

notes

10

On Diligence

The Lesson

就職第一課

Bodhi Light Tales
84 The Lesson

Scan me to listen!
掃我，聆聽故事!

Once upon a time, there lived a young lady named Sylvia. She recently graduated from college but was still unsure as to what she wanted to do in life. Under pressure[1] in having to pay her bills, Sylvia applied for a job as a personal assistant[2] in a finance company. Not long after submitting[3] her application, she was interviewed by Hugo, the General Manager, and got the job.

One month into her new job, Sylvia had received all the training required and was well-equipped[4] to perform her duties. One day, a man named Dominic arrived at the reception desk.

"Hello, how can I help you?" Sylvia asked.

"Hi, my name is Dominic. I'm here for an interview with Hugo Reynolds," Dominic said.

"Are you sure? I don't have you scheduled[5] in his calendar. Please wait, " Sylvia replied.

"I am sure, the appointment was booked for 1 p.m.," Dominic said.

"I'm sorry, it seems like I've double-

VOCABULARY

1. pressure (n.) 壓力
2. personal assistant (n.) 個人助理
3. submitting (v.) 提交
4. well-equipped (adj.) 設備齊全的
5. scheduled (v.) 預定；排定

　　有家公司剛聘任一位祕書，某天，公司來了一位想謀職的人，祕書隨即將此人帶到總經理辦公室，以待面試。總經理與這位求職者談了一陣子，即請祕書把客人送走。等祕書送走客人之後，總經理就問：

booked him for that time. Let me check if Hugo can still do the interview right now," Sylvia said.

"Okay, thank you," Dominic replied.

Without delay[6], Sylvia made a phone call. After a quick conversation[7], she said to Dominic, "Hugo is available for the interview. Can you please sign the guest form?"

After he'd completed the form, Sylvia brought Dominic to Hugo's office. Sylvia knocked on the door and she heard Hugo say, "Please come in."

Sylvia then signaled[8] for Dominic to enter. Hugo was already standing with his hand out for a handshake[9], "Nice to meet you," Hugo said.

"Nice to meet you too," Dominic replied.

"Please have a seat," Hugo said.

Sylvia then poured[10] a glass of water for

VOCABULARY

6. delay (n.) 耽擱
7. conversation (n.) 對話
8. signaled (v.) 示意
9. handshake (n.) 握手
10. poured (v.) 倒

「剛才那位前來求職的人，妳看他修養如何？」

「不認識，不知道。」

「妳覺得他的學識如何？」

「我不清楚。」

「他的能力，妳覺得怎麼樣？」

Dominic. Before she put the glass down on the table, Dominic had already raised[11] both of his hands to receive it and said to her warmly, "Thank you very much."

Sylvia nodded and left the room.

The interview ended fairly quickly. Hugo walked Dominic to the reception desk and said, "It was a pleasure[12] meeting you. We will contact[13] you in a few days. Have a good evening."

"Thank you very much. I look forward to hearing from you," Dominic replied.

As he was leaving, Hugo heard Dominic say to Sylvia, "Thank you for the glass of water. That was very kind of you. It really helped me settle down[14] for the interview."

"You're welcome. Before you leave, please sign off here."

After Dominic signed the form, he said, "Thank you again. Hope to see you soon."

Sylvia nodded and waved[15] goodbye. Then, her phone rang. It was Hugo asking her

VOCABULARY

11. raised (v.) 舉起
12. pleasure (n.) 愉快；榮幸
13. contact (v.) 聯絡
14. settle down (p.v.) 適應
15. waved (v.) 揮手

「沒有相處過，怎麼會知道呢？」祕書還是一付不知道的表情。

「他的為人，富責任心、忠貞感，妳覺得如何？」

「我一無所知。」

「剛才妳送他走的時候，他是歡喜地離開呢？還是抱怨、不滿地離開呢？」

to come to his office.

"Please send this out today. It's urgent[16]," Hugo said to Sylvia as he handed her an envelope.

"Will do," Sylvia replied.

"By the way, what do you think about Dominic?" Hugo asked.

"I don't know... I only just met him," Sylvia replied.

Hugo then asked, "What about his skills[17] and knowledge[18]? Do you think he is a good fit for this company?"

"I don't know... I didn't look at his resume[19]," Sylvia replied.

Hugo continued, "What about his character? Do you think he has potential[20]?"

"I don't know... I just welcomed him and brought him to your office. How can I judge a person based only on a few minutes of interaction?"

Hugo looked at Sylvia disappointedly and said "I expect, at the very least, for you

VOCABULARY

16. urgent (adj.) 緊急的
17. skills (n.) 技能
18. knowledge (n.) 學識；學問
19. resume (n.) 個人簡歷
20. potential (n.) 潛力；潛能

「我實在看不出來。」祕書搔搔腦說。

總經理面露嚴肅：「妳不能老是回答不知道、不知道，這世間上的任何事，都要知道才能做啊！什麼都不知道，妳該如何辦事？妳有眼睛可以看，妳有耳朵可以聽，面對周遭的人事物，必須有觀察力與判斷的能力。」

to give me some feedback on him, even if you've only met briefly. You didn't notice, or have any thoughts or feelings on how he thanked you personally for giving him a glass of water? It shows that not only is he polite but also thankful and compassionate. How many people do you know say thank you personally to a receptionist or an assistant, after an interview, for giving them a glass of water? You not noticing these details, and answering 'I don't know' to all my questions reveals to me, you have a rather careless and sloppy[21] attitude to your own job and responsibilities."

Stunned[22], Sylvia replied, "I thought my job was to greet visitors, make sure they get to where they need to go, and escort[23] them out."

Now looking even more disappointed, Hugo said, "Yes, those are your responsibilities as my assistant. But I expect more from you. I hope that you are mindful[24] and attentive[25] to everything that happens around you. If you don't pay close attention to details, then your

VOCABULARY

21. sloppy (adj.) 粗心的
22. stunned (adj.) 驚愕的
23. escort (v.) 護送
24. mindful (adj.) 覺察的
25. attentive (adj.) 關心的；照顧周到的

總經理的一席話，猶如禪師的棒喝，重重地打在祕書的心坎上，她如夢初醒，自此改變了她原有的處事態度和人生觀念。事後她告訴總經理：「感謝您的教誨，讓我上了人生最棒的一堂課。」

achievements will be rather limited. You have eyes and ears, use them wisely. Don't merely see but observe attentively. Don't just hear but listen closely. If you can use both keen[26] observation and awareness when doing your job and living your life, then I'm sure you'll have a successful future."

Hugo's words struck Sylvia like a lightning bolt. She said to Hugo, "You're right. I've been careless and inattentive. Thank you for teaching me a most valuable lesson."

This story highlights the importance of being mindful and aware. Like Sylvia, if we live our lives or do our jobs carelessly or unaware, then our ability to solve problems and face obstacles[27] will be limited. If we can train our senses and minds to perceive and process accordingly, then we'll be equipped to face and resolve[28] any challenges we may encounter.

Our friends, elders, and colleagues may teach us lessons we ought to listen to and learn from. If we are receptive[29] and open to their guidance, as we accumulate[30] lessons and wisdom from these

VOCABULARY

26. keen (adj.) 敏銳的
27. obstacles (n.) 阻礙
28. resolve (v.) 解決
29. receptive (adj.) 樂於接受的
30. accumulate (v.) 積累

慣於以「不知道」來應付回答，永遠無法解決問題。唯有啟動感官、思想，判斷一切事物，才能徹底解決問題。

experiences, we shall surely improve and better ourselves. Like Sylvia, she was appreciative of the lesson Hugo taught her. With a mindset of aspiring[31] to improve ourselves and cultivating our minds, we can transform ourselves and benefit society. If we are open-minded[32] and humble[33] in the face of advice and criticism[34] from others, we shall set ourselves on the path towards becoming a most capable and competent[35] person in whatever we do in our lives.

VOCABULARY

31. aspiring (v.) 渴望；有志於
32. open-minded (adj.) 開明的
33. humble (adj.) 謙虛的
34. criticism (n.) 批評；評論
35. competent (adj.) 能幹的

　　我們若能時時刻刻在朋友、長官、同事身上，不斷地以「我上了一課」的心態學習，把這每一課寶貴的經驗、智慧累積起來，改進自己，昇華心靈，將來我們必定是一個人格健全、虛心受教、有大用的能人。

Dharma Words by Venerable Master Hsing Yun

In the pursuit of learning, maintain a joyful attitude.
In the face of advice, keep an open mind.
In taking on responsibility, show courage.
In dealing with others, remain respectful.

星雲大師法語

上課聞道要有歡喜心,
指導訓話要有接受心,
做事擔當要有勇敢心,
和人相處要有恭敬心。

notes

11

On Diligence

Heavy Bag

還重嗎？

Bodhi Light Tales
85 Heavy Bag

Scan me to listen!
掃我，聆聽故事!

Once upon a time, there lived a Korean Seon Master named Kyong Ho. He began studying sutras at the age of fourteen. By the time he was twenty-three, he had already mastered all the major sutras. Master Kyong Ho played a vital[1] role in Korean Buddhism, and together with his disciples[2] was committed[3] to propagating[4] the Dharma.

One day, Master Kyong Ho was on his way to a town with his disciple to give a Dharma talk. On the way, the disciple kept complaining about how heavy his bag was. Whining nonstop, he muttered[5], "Why do we need to carry so much with us? Why can't we just travel light?"

The Master said, "We need to bring books for our Dharma brothers."

"But this bag is so heavy… Can we take a rest please?" the disciple replied.

"We've just started our journey, we shall rest later. If we keep taking breaks, we'll be late or even miss the talk," the Master said as

VOCABULARY

1. vital (adj.) 重要的
2. disciples (n.) 弟子
3. committed (v.) 忠於；投入
4. propagating (v.) 傳播
5. muttered (v.) 喃喃低語

　　韓國的鏡虛禪師，帶著出家不久的弟子滿空法師出外行腳布教，弟子一路上滿腹牢騷，嘀咕不停，嫌背的行李太重，不斷地要求師父找個地方休息。鏡虛禪師卻說路途那麼遙遠，老是休息，什麼時候才能達到目地的呢？鏡虛禪師仍然精神飽滿，逕自向前走去。

he continued walking.

Moaning[6] and groaning[7], the disciple dragged[8] himself to follow behind his Master.

Not long after, they arrived at a small village. Walking past the market, they met a beautiful woman walking towards them with a water jug perched on her head. As she came closer, the Master leaned toward her and muttered something. The woman screamed, dropped the water jug, and it shattered[9] into pieces. Everyone at the market heard the commotion[10] and was frightened. One of the villagers waved his stick at the Master and yelled, "Hey you! What did you say to the lady?"

Without replying, the Master ran away as fast as he could. Behind him, the disciple saw his Master running away, and ran after

VOCABULARY

6. moaning (v.) 悲嘆
7. groaning (v.) 嘆息
8. dragged (v.) 拖拽
9. shattered (v.) 打碎
10. commotion (n.) 騷動

有一日，師徒倆經過一座村莊，迎面遇到一位姿態美麗的婦女，走在前面的師父不曉得跟那位婦女說了些什麼，只見那女人突然大聲尖叫。婦女的家人和鄰居聞聲出來一看，以為和尚輕薄婦女，齊聲喊打。身材高大的鏡虛禪師不顧一切地向前奔逃，走在後面背著行李的徒弟也跟隨師父快速往前飛奔。

him.

After a while, the Master looked behind him to make sure they were safe and the villagers were nowhere in sight[11]. Reaching a crossroad[12], he stopped and turned around to wait for the disciple.

After the disciple had caught up to his master, out of breath, he said, "Are we safe?"

The Master nodded[13], patting[14] him on the shoulder, and asked, "How goes it with the bag? Is it still heavy? You just ran over five miles carrying it."

"Master, all I could think of was not to get caught. So no, I did not even feel the weight of the bag when I was running!!!" the disciple replied.

The Master laughed and said, "Now, our journey is back on schedule[15]. We might even have extra time to now take a rest!"

Only then did the disciple realize why his Master had made them run.

VOCABULARY

11. sight (n.) 視線
12. crossroad (n.) 交叉路
13. nodded (v.) 點頭示意
14. patting (v.) 輕拍
15. on schedule (phrase) 準時

　　跑過幾條山路後，鏡虛禪師見村人無法追上，就在一條寂靜的山路邊停了下來，回頭看徒弟氣喘噓噓地跑了過來，就問徒弟道：「剛才背了那麼多行李，跑了這麼遠的路，還覺得重嗎？」

　　「師父！很奇怪，剛才奔跑的時候，一點都不覺得行李很重！」

This story teaches us that having goals can motivate[16] us to overcome the obstacles we face on our path to success. In this story, the disciple overcame the burden of his heavy bag after realizing he did not want to be caught by the villagers. This became his goal, and he was determined to succeed. Similarly, on our journey in life, if we set goals and maintain a strong determination to succeed, then our inner strength will grow as a result. Even if we are faced with challenges or obstacles, we will have the courage to face them and move forward.

Similarly, a person with big dreams can go a long way. Bodhisattvas, with their great compassion, have the power and resolve[17] to help countless sentient beings[18], and yet their bodies and minds never feel tired.

The journey in the cycle of life and rebirth is long and endless. Only if we aspire[19] to firm vows can we transcend[20] time and space,

VOCABULARY

16. motivate (v.) 驅使；激勵
17. resolve (n.) 決心；堅決
18. sentient beings (n.) 眾生
19. aspire (v.) 追求；有志於
20. transcend (v.) 超越

不覺得行李重，是因為心中有不顧一切向前奔馳的目標。在人生的旅途上，如果對前途沒有堅毅不拔的信心及目標，內心就生不起力量，無法負擔繁重難關的挑戰。人因夢想而遠大，菩薩更因大悲心生起大勢力，能廣度無邊的眾生，身心不覺疲累。

and reach the state of a bodhisattva. All bodhisattvas have made great vows to liberate[21] living beings without discrimination[22]. If we can be like the bodhisattvas, no matter how heavy the "bags" we carry in our lives may be, we shall accept and tolerate whatever life throws at us. By cultivating our minds and willingly accepting responsibility, all our burdens will feel as light as a feather[23] and be handled with ease.

VOCABULARY

21. liberate (v.) 解放；使解脫
22. discrimination (n.) 歧視
23. feather (n.) 羽毛

生死路途遙遠，唯有心中立下堅固志願，爾後方能盡虛空遍法界，令一切眾生之類入無餘涅槃，而心中無人我與無眾生之相。生命的行李沉重嗎？只要你能當下承當，再沉重的生命包袱，也可以輕如鴻毛。

Dharma Words by Venerable Master Hsing Yun

Determination helps you reach your goal.
Perseverance leads to success.

星雲大師法語

決心可以使人不致半途而廢,
毅力可以使人走上成功之路。

notes

12

On Diligence

Laziness Is Your Downfall

懶惰之害

Bodhi Light Tales
99 Laziness Is Your Downfall

Scan me to listen!
掃我,聆聽故事!

Once upon a time, there lived the king of all hells named Yama. In East Asian and Buddhist mythology[1], Yama was a wrathful[2] god who presided[3] over all hells, the cycle of rebirth[4], and judged the dead.

One day, Yama was dealing with a case of human rebirth. He called out, "Do we have a Gasper here?"

"Yes, I'm here!" Gasper replied.

As Yama looked through Gasper's case file, he said, "You've served your time here, it is time for you to be reborn as a human being."

Gasper shook his head and said, "No, I don't want to be reborn as a human being. Living as a human being was hard, especially since I was poor. I always worried every day about having enough money to live. Each day was hard work, all just to stay alive. I don't want to go through all that suffering[5] again. Would it be possible for me not to be reborn as a human being, please?"

"Do not worry, I have looked at your history.

VOCABULARY

1. mythology (n.) 神話
2. wrathful (adj.) 憤怒的;激怒的
3. presided (v.) 統轄
4. rebirth (n.) 重生;投生
5. suffering (n.) 痛苦

閻羅王對一個小鬼說:「你可以投胎做人了!」小鬼搖頭說:「做人啊,我可不要去,人間很苦的,尤其是貧窮人,衣食不全,天天為了三餐住宿而煩惱,太辛苦了。」閻羅王安慰小鬼:「你放心,我看過你的因緣簿了,這一次你會有高達一萬兩黃金的財產,足以讓你舒服度日,高枕無憂的。」小鬼得到閻羅王的保證,也就放心投胎去了。

As a human being, you were quite generous⁶. So, for your new life, you will be given a sum⁷ of money! That should help you get a head start and assure⁸ you a comfortable life," Yama explained.

"Really? How much money will I receive?" Gasper asked.

"You will be given $100,000," Yama replied.

Now reassured⁹, Gasper agreed to be reborn once again as a human being.

Not long after, Gasper was reborn into a loving family. His parents adored him and gave him a good education. However, Gasper was ever-changing¹⁰. He studied hard for a few years but then was bored. So, he decided to drop out of school to learn martial arts. Before

VOCABULARY

6. generous (adj.) 慷慨的
7. sum (n.) 總數；總和
8. assure (v.) 向……保證
9. reassured (v.) 使安心
10. ever-changing (adj.) 千變萬化的

出世的小鬼，父母親百般疼愛，還送他到學堂讀書，可是讀沒幾年，他便吵著要學武，武藝未成，他覺得沒意思，就改做生意，經營一陣子，錢都還沒賺到，又跑去務農，這一回兒，他還是三天捕魚五天晒網，還不待收成，就餓死在田裡了。小鬼死後，心有不甘地找閻羅王理論：「你說我會有一萬兩黃金的財產，可是你看看，我最後還是餓死在田地。」

he had completed his martial arts training, he changed his mind again. He felt learning martial arts was useless, thinking, "Self-defense[11] won't earn me money. All these bruises[12] from training are not worth the effort." So, he decided to start a business. A couple of months later, Gasper barely[13] made any profit and didn't even break even. Since he'd made little profit, he decided to close down his business. He then turned to farming, deciding to work in the fields after hearing from a friend about the thriving[14] business of agriculture.

Farming was nothing like what Gasper had imagined. He was always exhausted, so he would work three days and rest for five days. Unfortunately, before he could harvest anything, he died while working in the fields.

When Gasper appeared again before Yama, he was furious[15] and said, "You told me I would receive $100,000 upon being reborn as a human being, but I received nothing. You lied to me! I tried to make a living, but it was

VOCABULARY

11. self-defense (n.) 自衛
12. bruises (n.) 瘀傷
13. barely (adv.) 幾乎沒有
14. thriving (adj.) 欣欣向榮的
15. furious (adj.) 狂怒的

聽了小鬼的冤屈，閻羅王趕緊命鬼卒去查，才知道那一萬兩黃金是交給土地公的。閻羅王把土地公找來，質問道：「你把黃金拿到哪裡去了？」土地公趕快解釋：「向閻羅王報告，因為他要讀書，我就把一萬兩黃金交給文昌帝君，讓他好好地讀書，將來考上狀元。」

too hard. It is your fault[16] that I died working in the fields."

Puzzled, Yama replied, "I prepared[17] the money for you. But why did you not receive it? I will look into it and get to the bottom of this." Yama then ordered one of his assistants to gather everyone involved[18] in Gasper's rebirth.

The assistant reported to Yama, "It appears that the money due was given to the God of the Earth." He then called for the God of the Earth to come forward.

"What did you do with the money for Gasper?" Yama asked.

"Please allow me to explain. I did have the money ready for Gasper, but since he was studying at the time, I gave the money to the God of Literature. We both agreed[19] to give him the money when he became a scholar."

The assistant then called upon[20] the God of Literature to come forward.

"What happened with the money for Gasper?" Yama asked.

VOCABULARY

16. fault (n.) 過錯；過失
17. prepared (v.) 準備
18. involved (v.) 牽涉
19. agreed (v.) 同意
20. called upon (p.v.) 請

閻羅王把文昌帝君找來，問：「這個人的一萬兩黃金呢？」文昌帝君說：「一萬兩黃金正準備給他運用時，他又要去學武，我就把黃金交給武曲星君。」

閻羅王再把武曲星君找來。武曲星君回答：「本來要給他用的，誰知道沒幾年，他說要去學做生意，我便把錢交給財神。」

"The money was ready, but when I was about to give it to him, he changed his mind and began learning martial arts[21]. So, I gave the money to the God of Martial Arts."

Yama repeated[22] his question to the God of Martial Arts, who replied, "Yes, the money was ready for him. But then he decided to start a business. So I gave the money to the God of Wealth."

When the God of Wealth came forward, Yama asked him, "Why didn't you help Gasper make a good profit[23]?"

The God of Wealth replied, "Before I could help him, he quit[24] after only two months. He then decided to become a farmer. So, I gave the money to the God of the Soil."

Yama then questioned the God of the Soil, who replied, "King Yama, the one at fault is Gasper. He put no effort into cultivating[25] the fields. Before the money could reach him, he starved to death in the field."

Yama sighed and felt sorry. After a

VOCABULARY

21. martial arts (n.) 武術
22. repeated (v.) 重複；複述
23. profit (n.) 利潤；盈利
24. quit (v.) 辭職；放棄
25. cultivating (v.) 耕作；栽培

閻羅王只得再把財神找來：「你怎麼不讓他賺錢呢？」「他才剛開張幾天，就跑去務農啦。」

最後，把神農大帝找來，神農大帝說：「閻羅王，是他自己不肯種田，錢還沒用上，就餓死在田裡啦！所以錢還在我這裡。」

「唉！」閻羅王嘆了口氣，說：「懶惰不能成功，命中雖有錢，還是得靠勤勞精進才有所得！」

moment of silence, he said, "Laziness does not lead to success. Though Gasper was destined[26] to receive money, he did not work for it. One must be diligent and work hard to harvest."

Yama called Gasper to come forward, and said, "Laziness is your downfall. You were destined to have money, but you did not receive it because you did not work for it. You have no one to blame[27] but yourself."

Gasper, humbled[28], kept quiet and simply nodded.

This story highlights the danger of laziness. One cannot expect results without working hard to realize[29] them. As the saying goes, "There's no such thing as a free lunch." Simply put, one cannot expect something for nothing. If we are not willing to work hard, and simply wait or expect for things to happen, we will achieve[30] nothing.

Another example illustrates this. Once, there lived a farmer who worked hard in the field. Suddenly he heard a loud noise. A rabbit had hit a nearby tree and died due to a broken neck. The farmer brought

VOCABULARY

26. destined (adj.) 命定的
27. blame (v.) 責備；責怪
28. humbled (v.) 使……感到自慚
29. realize (v.) 實現
30. achieve (v.) 完成；達到

閻羅王所言甚是，即使命中注定有財有富，坐著等待也坐吃山空，不知勤勞耕耘，等同守株待兔，守到葉枯朽、樹傾倒，還是一無所獲。

the dead rabbit home and cooked it. That night, he thought, "I don't need to work hard anymore. I just need to sit by that tree every day and wait for a rabbit to hit it." From then on, he stopped working and simply waited for the rabbit. However, since that day, he never saw another rabbit again and his field turned into a wasteland[31]. This reminds[32] us that if we do nothing but wait for a lucky break, nothing is what awaits us at the end.

VOCABULARY

31. wasteland (n.) 荒地
32. reminds (v.) 提醒

Dharma Words by Venerable Master Hsing Yun

Ignorance and wrong thoughts bring bad karma.
Laziness and negligence ruin careers.
Blaming yourself is useless.
Whining and blaming others make things worse.

星雲大師法語

愚癡邪見即是自造惡業，
懶惰懈怠就是自毀前程，
自怨自艾終究於事無補，
怨天尤人只會更加壞事。

notes

13

On Diligence

A Mother's Love

背母親

Bodhi Light Tales
100 A Mother's Love

Scan me to listen!
掃我,聆聽故事!

Once upon a time, there lived a single mother named Anna, and her son, Joe. Anna always worried about Joe, as he was rebellious[1] and spent all of his time with his friends. Anna tried very hard to convince[2] Joe about making the right kind of friends. However, Joe refused to listen.

One late evening, as Joe was about to head out, Anna said, "You're still going outside this late?"

Uncalled for, Joe angrily replied, "Stop controlling me!" He grabbed his backpack and stormed out of the house.

Dumbfounded[3], Anna sat in the living room, wondering about Joe and his angry outburst[4]. She stayed up waiting for him all night, but he never came home.

The next morning, Anna went into Joe's room and found a note on his desk. The note said, "I am leaving home for good." Barely comprehending[5] the words and overcome by her emotions, Anna burst into tears, gripping

VOCABULARY

1. rebellious (adj.) 叛逆的
2. convince (v.) 說服
3. dumbfounded (adj.) 目瞪口呆的
4. outburst (n.) 爆發
5. comprehending (v.) 理解

有一位母親因為兒子的叛逆，日日憂心。縱使她費盡唇舌勸導，仍然挽回不了兒子浪蕩的心；不肖的兒子對母親的苦心不但不領情，還認為母親太過保守，束縛他的自由，於是決定離家出走。母親面對兒子的離家，又音信杳然，傷心欲絕，終日以淚洗面。時日久了，竟哭瞎了雙眼。

the note with both hands.

Every day since, Anna looked for Joe everywhere but never found him. For months, she lived with mixed feelings of anger, sadness, and anxiety[6]. She missed[7] Joe very much and cried nonstop every time she thought of him. Eventually, she cried so much that she began to lose her eyesight.

One day, Anna was listening to the news and heard that Joe had been arrested[8] for stealing a car. When she found out which prison he'd been sent to, she decided to visit him.

Upon seeing Joe, Anna burst into tears. As they were separated[9] by a glass partition[10], Anna quickly picked up the phone and signaled Joe to do the same. But Joe refused to make eye contact. Keeping his head down, he picked up

VOCABULARY

6. anxiety (n.) 掛念；憂慮
7. missed (v.) 想念
8. arrested (v.) 逮捕
9. separated (v.) 分開
10. partition (n.) 隔牆

　　幾年後，母親輾轉得到兒子入獄的消息，因為掛念兒子，想盡了辦法到監獄探望。探監時，由於隔了一道玻璃，思子心切的母親請求讓她能夠摸摸兒子的頭，辦事人員感動一個母親的愛心，就成全她的心願。母親摸著兒子的頭，一直鼓勵他日後要改過向善，然而頑強的兒子仍不為所動。

the phone and said, "Hello…"

"I missed you so much! I looked everywhere for you!" Anna desperately[11] said.

"Mum… I…" Joe mumbled[12].

"I know, you don't need to say a thing," Anna replied with her hand on the glass partition. She wished she could hug Joe to let him know how much she still loved him. Turning to the officer on duty, she asked, "Is it okay for me to give my son a hug? I haven't seen or heard from him for over a year. All I want to do is just hug him."

The officer on duty felt the pain and love written all over Anna's face, and agreed to let them meet face to face. They were brought to another room, and when Anna saw Joe again, she hugged him tightly. She whispered[13] to him, "You're still my good boy. You can do better than this…"

Joe kept silent and nodded.

When visiting time was over, Anna stumbled[14] getting up and struggled[15] to find her bag. Looking at his mother, Joe suddenly

VOCABULARY

11. desperately (adv.) 拚命地
12. mumbled (v.) 咕噥
13. whispered (v.) 耳語
14. stumbled (v.) 絆倒
15. struggled (v.) 掙扎

終於，談話時間結束了，兒子看到母親摸索著準備離去的身影，心中生起不忍，他向辦事人請求，背著瞎眼的母親到大門，送她乘上計程車。辦事人員因為他在獄中沒有不良的紀錄，也就沒有為難他。

realized that her eyesight had deteriorated[16]. So, he asked the officer in charge if he could help his mother to the front gate and into a taxi home. The officer knew of Joe's good behavior and conduct[17] history as a prisoner, so he nodded and said, "OK, I'll keep an eye on you but please keep this quiet and keep it short."

Joe smiled at the officer and said, "Thank you so much."

He then turned to his mother, held her hand, and said, "Mother, please let me carry you to the entrance and get you a taxi home." Joe then got down on his knees so she could hold on to his back.

As they made their way to the front gate, Anna smiled and said to Joe, "This is the happiest moment[18] of my life. When you were little, you were so afraid of the dark each night, I struggled to put you to sleep. But as soon as I carried you on my back, you fell asleep. So every night, I lulled[19] you to sleep by giving you a piggyback[20] ride. Now, you are the one giving

VOCABULARY

16. deteriorated (v.) 惡化
17. conduct (n.) 行為；舉止
18. moment (n.) 時刻；時候
19. lulled (v.) 使發困
20. piggyback (n.) 背；馱

兒子背著母親，走在監獄的通道上，母親對兒子說：「這一刻是我一生最快樂的時候。想起你小的時候，晚上怕黑，媽媽也是這樣背你，哄著你入睡；今天你能背媽媽，媽媽感到很欣慰，就是死了也沒有什麼遺

me a piggyback ride. If I were to die right now, it would be perfect."

"Please don't say that," Joe replied worriedly.

After that day, Joe reflected[21] on his mother's visit and decided to turn over a new leaf[22]. While serving his remaining time in prison, he enrolled in many courses. After his release[23], he worked hard to get into college and eventually graduated with flying colors[24]. He then started his own business and eventually became successful[25].

VOCABULARY

21. reflected (v.) 深思
22. turn over a new leaf (idiom) 改過自新
23. release (n.) 釋放
24. with flying colors (idiom) 成績優異
25. successful (adj.) 成功的

憾了！」兒子被母親的話感動，回憶起母親養育的辛勞，從此洗心革面，在獄中發憤讀書，出獄後更考上一流的大學，成為社會上能幹有為的青年。

This story highlights the love of a mother. It was Anna's love that touched Joe, making him realize he could be better. This story is a great example of how love can change a person for the better.

Deep down, all of us have a pure and kind heart. No one is born evil. However, many of us lose our way as we get caught up in the web of our selfish and wicked[26] desires. When we are driven and influenced by evil desires, our minds are clouded and we're trapped[27] in a vicious[28] circle. We cannot see clearly, nor are we aware of the impacts of our actions. As a result, we are enslaved[29] by our own desires, unable to escape them. If we can realize this and always strive to be a better person, then we shall find the means to liberate ourselves. In other words, let us transform our troublesome mind into a mind of repentance[30], and turn our angry mind into a mind of gratitude.

VOCABULARY

26. wicked (adj.) 惡劣的
27. trapped (v.) 被困
28. vicious (adj.) 惡性的
29. enslaved (v.) 束縛
30. repentance (n.) 懺悔

不肖的兒子由於母親慈悲愛語，終於使他幡然醒悟，棄暗投明。人，原本也有一顆良善純淨的心，由於外在欲望的鉤牽，使我們被世間的牢獄囚禁，不得出離。

換心改性，才是我們解脫的因緣。聰明的人兒！把我們剛強的心，改成慚愧的心，把怨恨的心，改成感恩的心吧！

Dharma Words by Venerable Master Hsing Yun

Transform your loved ones with virtue.
Guide them with morality.
Help them with kindness to succeed.
Wish them blessings.

星雲大師法語

要用倫理淨化所愛,
要用道德領航所愛,
要用善美成就所愛,
要用祝福加持所愛。

14

On Diligence

The Squashed "Frog"

茄子喻

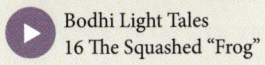

Scan me to listen!
掃我，聆聽故事!

Once upon a time, there was a novice monk named Han. In a monastery, someone must rise early to sound the wake-up board signals. And for this particular week, it was Han's duty to wake everybody up.

One night, after a long day, Han was on his way back to his dormitory[1]. Feeling exhausted[2], Han decided to take a shortcut through the garden. Though the stars were shining and the fragrance[3] of the flowers would usually have brought joy to Han, that night, he just wanted to get back to his room as quickly as possible.

Soon, he arrived at the gate of his dormitory, and as he stepped through, he felt something soft and squishy[4] under his foot.

"Oh my! What was that?" Han thought to himself.

Now confused and afraid, not knowing what to do, Han ran as fast as he could until he reached his room.

Still pondering[5] over what he had stepped on, he whispered to himself, "Could it be a frog?

VOCABULARY

1. dormitory (n.) 宿舍
2. exhausted (adj.) 筋疲力盡的
3. fragrance (n.) 芬芳
4. squishy (adj.) 黏糊糊的
5. pondering (v.) 沉思；默想

話說寺廟裡晚上都安排有晚課，某一夜，小沙彌做完晚課後，走回寮房。由於夜色昏暗，走著、走著，小沙彌忽然驚覺腳下踩到軟軟的東西，他心想：「糟了！我可能踩死一隻青蛙。」這一整個晚上，小沙彌心裡很難過，根本睡不著，不斷唉聲嘆氣地自責：「我怎麼這麼不小心，踩死一條生命啊？」

Oh please not..."

For the rest of the night, Han was overwhelmed[6] with fear and remorse[7]. He couldn't stop thinking about the soft and squishy thing that he had stepped on. His thought even went to his precepts as a Buddhist monk. Most particularly, the precept of refraining from killing. He felt terrible[8] that he had broken his precepts.

"I should have taken the normal route instead of the shortcut. How could I have been so careless? And just like that, I took a life," he blamed himself over and over again.

Eventually, Han managed to fall asleep. Because of his guilt, he dreamt that he was being chased[9] by thousands of frogs claiming for his own life. Waking up in a cold sweat, he thought, "What a nightmare! I need to tell Master what I have done."

Now up at the break of dawn, Han quickly got ready and went to see his Master.

"Master, I need to confess[10] something

VOCABULARY

6. overwhelmed (v.) 不知所措
7. remorse (n.) 後悔；懊悔
8. terrible (adj.) 糟糕的
9. chased (v.) 追逐
10. confess (v.) 供認；承認

第二天，天剛亮，小沙彌趕緊跑出去，想去埋葬青蛙。當他來到昨晚經過的地方，看到一條被踩爛的茄子，不禁鬆了一口氣，說：「還好！還好！原來是茄子，不是青蛙。」事情真相大白之後，一整晚的焦慮、痛苦，霎時消失得無影無蹤。

佛教常說凡事要講清楚、弄明白，因為不說清楚、不太明白，常常容易曲解別人的意思，模糊事實，使得人與人之間產生誤會。而這些誤會、顛倒、曲解，

awful. I took a life. Last night, on my way to my room, I stepped on something soft and squishy, it was a frog... I killed it! I feel horrible. Then, I dreamt that frogs were coming after me seeking[11] to take my life. I feel terrible about what happened. What should I do?" cried Han.

"Stay calm, how about we find the frog and give it a proper burial[12]," said the Master.

Han and his Master went to find the frog. They followed the route that Han took the night before, and searched everywhere, but they just couldn't find any trace[13] of the frog.

However, there was one thing lying on the ground. It was a squashed eggplant.

"Look! I think last night it was an overripe[14] eggplant that you stepped on!" exclaimed the Master.

Han let out a big sigh of relief[15] and muttered, "Thank Buddha! It was an eggplant, not a frog."

VOCABULARY

11. seeking (v.) 尋求；試圖
12. burial (n.) 埋葬
13. trace (n.) 痕跡；蹤跡
14. overripe (adj.) 過熟的
15. relief (n.) 如釋重負；輕鬆

會讓我們心裡升起煩惱，甚至做出傷害別人的行為。所以，凡事講清楚、弄明白，是很重要的。

該如何講清楚、弄明白呢？就要靠智慧來辨別。譬如：小沙彌晚上看不清楚，誤解了事實，等到天亮之後，才發現不是他想像中那麼一回事。所以，智慧好比日光一般，人生旅程上有了智慧，任何的事情，才能夠照澈，才能夠看得清楚明白，因此智慧是何等重要啊！

Han realized he had spent all night feeling upset about something he didn't do. And just like that, all his worries and fears went away.

In the story, Han was misled by his misconceived[16] truth, and only after realizing what really happened, he was relieved from his anxieties and worries. How often do we make things up and make assumptions[17]? Just like Han let his troubles affect him, causing unnecessary worry and fear.

When we are unclear or unsure about something, we often mistake someone's good intentions or misinterpret[18] reality. This can create misunderstandings among one another. These kinds of misunderstandings not only produce unnecessary defilements, sometimes even more serious and harmful actions can be caused.

There's a saying, "There is no impartial[19] world. When worry, alarm, and regret conquer[20] the mind, the world becomes very subjective."

VOCABULARY

16. misconceived (adj.) 誤解的
17. assumptions (n.) 假設；臆斷
18. misinterpret (v.) 曲解
19. impartial (adj.) 公平的；公正的
20. conquer (v.) 征服；戰勝

當我們有了困擾，或對某人產生不諒解時，更需要平心靜氣地以智慧來觀察。有時，把情緒擺一旁，事情看清楚後，反而一切的陰霾都會消失無蹤。

奉勸大家多看佛書，多聽經聞法，乃至於閱讀有益身心的書籍，這些都可以增加我們的智慧，減少心中的煩惱。

Dharma Words by Venerable Master Hsing Yun

To see right, our eyes must look past illusions.
To hear right, our ears must listen with care.
To speak right, our mouth must tell no lies.
To do right, our hands must shun evil.
To walk right, our feet must find the path.
To think right, our mind must discern the truth.

星雲大師法語

眼欲看，當看其邪與正。
耳欲聽，當聽其是與非。
口欲言，當言其對與錯。
手欲做，當做其真與假。
腳欲行，當行其當與否。
心欲想，當想其善與惡。

15

On Diligence

The Diligent Little Dog

小狗也會說話

Bodhi Light Tales
188 The Diligent Little Dog

Scan me to listen!
掃我，聆聽故事!

Once upon a time, in a quaint[1] little village, there lived a family who had a special companion—a little dog named Charlie. This family was known for their laziness, and every day, when household chores needed to be done, they would find ways to avoid[2] them. The mother would ask the father to take care of things, but he too was equally lazy, and instead, he would pass the responsibilities onto their children. Unfortunately, the children were more interested in playing and having fun than doing household chores, leaving everything undone.

Seeing the chaos and mess that accumulated[3] in their cozy[4] little house, Charlie the dog felt a deep sense of concern for his family. Although he could not understand human words, he understood their actions quite well. It broke his little heart to see them struggling[5] to keep their home tidy and happy.

One sunny morning, as the family lazed around, Charlie bravely stepped forward and

VOCABULARY

1. quaint (adj.) 別緻的
2. avoid (v.) 避開；逃避
3. accumulated (v.) 積累；積聚
4. cozy (adj.) 溫馨的；溫暖舒適的
5. struggling (v.) 掙扎

話說，有一戶人家生性懶惰，每日的家事，媽媽不做就叫爸爸做，爸爸也懶惰不願意做，就叫兒女做，兒女貪玩不肯做，就叫小狗做。小狗不得辦法，只好挑起大梁，打理家務。牠用尾巴掃地，用身體抹桌椅，甚至用嘴啣水管澆花草，把家整理得潔淨雅觀。

decided to take on the role of the family caretaker. With determination in his eyes, he used his wagging[6] tail as a makeshift broom, sweeping the dirt and dust out of every corner of the house. His furry body became a cleaning cloth as he wiped the tables and chairs clean, determined to make the place look neat and tidy.

But Charlie did not stop there. He noticed the flowers and plants in the house were looking droopy[7] and in need of water. So, with ingenuity[8] and resourcefulness[9], he carried a water hose in his mouth and carefully watered each and every one of them. The once unkempt[10] house started to sparkle with cleanliness and charm, thanks to

VOCABULARY

6. wagging (v.) 擺動
7. droopy (adj.) 下垂的
8. ingenuity (n.) 心靈手巧
9. resourcefulness (n.) 足智多謀
10. unkempt (adj.) 不整潔的；凌亂的

　　一天，客人登門拜訪，見到小狗在做家事，不禁詫異萬分：「哇！這麼能幹，連小狗也會做家事呀！」

　　小狗無奈地搖搖頭，說：「沒有辦法，他們都不做，我只好承擔起來。」

Charlie's hard work and selflessness.

One day, a kind guest came to visit their home. As the guest entered, he could not believe his eyes! There was the little dog, diligently doing household chores. "Wow! This is incredible[11]! Even the little dog knows how to do household chores!" the guest exclaimed[12] in amazement[13].

The little dog, trying to hide his exhaustion, could only shake his head helplessly and replied, "There's no other choice. They all refuse to do their part, so I have to take it upon myself."

The guest was taken aback and could not believe his ears. Looking at Charlie, he asked in disbelief, "Wait, did you just talk?"

Quickly realizing the potential consequences[14], the clever Charlie gestured[15] to the guest to hush and whispered, "Shhh! Please don't let them know I can speak, or else they might ask me to answer the phone too!"

VOCABULARY

11. incredible (adj.) 難以置信的
12. exclaimed (v.) 呼喊
13. amazement (n.) 驚奇
14. consequences (n.) 後果
15. gestured (v.) 手勢

客人一聽，大吃一驚：「小狗也會說話！」

小狗趕快對客人示意：「噓！不要讓他們知道我會說話，否則他們還會要我接電話呢！」

The guest chuckled softly at Charlie's wit and agreed to keep his secret. He was deeply moved by the little dog's dedication to his family and how he was willing to go above and beyond to help them.

As the days passed, Charlie continued to be the unsung[16] hero of the household, working tirelessly to keep the home a warm and cozy place. The family began to notice the changes and felt a newfound appreciation for their loyal companion.

This story teaches the harm of laziness. Depicted through this exaggerated[17] story, it carries significant messages. In life, whether it is work, studying, self-cultivation, or any other endeavor[18], the "spirit of diligence" is an indispensable[19] element. Consider this, if one merely plans but lacks diligence, working actively only three days out of five, they will forever remain stagnant[20]. A Buddhist text, the *Mahāprajñāpāramitā-śāstra*, points out, "Indolence destroys a laity's wealth, blessings, and welfare. It also destroys a monastic's chance of being reborn in

VOCABULARY

16. unsung (adj.) 未得到讚揚的
17. exaggerated (adj.) 誇張的
18. endeavor (n.) 努力
19. indispensable (adj.) 必不可少的；必需的
20. stagnant (adj.) 停滯的；不發展的

懶惰之害，透過誇張的寓言故事表現，極具意味。人生當中，舉凡就業工作、讀書學習、立身修道等等，「精進力」都是一項不可或缺的要素。想想，如果一味訂定計畫，卻是三天晒網二天捕魚，不具精進力，永遠也只是原地踏步罷了。因此《大智度論》舉出：「懈怠，破在家人財利、福利，破出家人生天樂、涅槃樂。」懈怠之害，害人匪淺。

the bliss of the heavens and the joy of Nirvana." The harm of indolence is not to be underestimated[21].

Throughout history, the wisdom and teachings of great saints and sages have all conveyed[22] the same message: with diligence, there is nothing that cannot be accomplished! There are a few texts that elaborate[23] on this:

- The *Sutra on the Mahayana Practice of the Six Perfections* states, "All worldly fruits and results arise from diligence."

- In *Zuo's Commentary*, it states that "The people's livelihood depends on diligence; with diligence, there will be no poverty."

- Han Yu in his work, *Explanation Upon Entering the Academy*, remarked, "Study excels with diligence and becomes neglected with play."

Therefore, to accomplish[24] a task or achieve an ideal[25], one must diligently practice and apply themselves.

VOCABULARY

21. underestimated (v.) 低估；輕視
22. conveyed (v.) 傳達
23. elaborate (v.) 詳盡說明；闡述
24. accomplish (v.) 完成；實現
25. ideal (n.) 理想

　　一件事要能辦成，理想要能實現，就必須勤於實踐，用功精進。《大乘理趣六波羅蜜多經》說：「世間諸果實，皆由精進生。」《左傳》則言：「民生在勤，勤則不匱。」韓愈在《進學解》中也說：「業精於勤，荒於嬉。」古今大德先賢留存的智慧法語，無不在告訴我們：精進則無事不辦！

Dharma Words by Venerable Master Hsing Yun

Self-construction is developing one's potential and
expanding one's horizons.
Self-destruction is laziness, indolence, and
unwillingness to form affinities with others.
Self-respect is accomplishing oneself
while benefiting others.
Self-annihilation is causing harm to others
while glorifying oneself.

星雲大師法語

開發潛能，更新觀念，這是自我建設。
懶惰懈怠，不結人緣，這是自我破壞。
成就自己，造福別人，這是自我尊重。
打擊別人，榮耀自己，這是自我毀滅。

notes

notes

notes

Credits 致謝

The Bodhi Light Tales were initially published on the Bodhi Light Tales Anchor podcast channel. We would like to express our heartfelt gratitude to everyone for their dedicated efforts.

《星雲說喻》最初以英文有聲書形式於 Anchor 播客平台推出，為「菩提心燈」系列故事。今結集成冊，特此感謝製作團隊的付出。

Editor-in-Chief 主編：
Venerable Miao Guang 妙光法師

Project Manager 專案執行：
Venerable Zhi Sheng 知笙法師

English Translators 英文翻譯：
Venerable Zhi Sheng 知笙法師
Belinda Hsueh 薛瑋瑩
Angela Ho 何慧玲

English Editors 英文編輯：
Arthur van Sevendonck
Jennifer Hsu 許嫡娟
Jenny Liu

Vocabulary Assistants 中英詞彙表整理：
Kathryn Lee 李苑嫣
Belinda Hsueh 薛瑋瑩
Handayani Fu

English Story Proofreaders 英文故事校稿：
Venerable Zu Dao 祖道法師
Arthur van Sevendonck
Kathryn Lee 李苑嫣
Jayme Long

Logo & Graphic Designer 平面設計：
Sedona Garcia

Illustrators (In order of illustrations contributed)
繪圖（按圖次序）：
Venerable Dao Pu 道璞法師
Venerable Youji 有紀法師
Venerable Neng Hui 能輝法師
Jack Yu 游智光
Lo Wan-ching 羅婉菁
Jonathon Cheung
Shi Jinhui 施金輝
Sedona Garcia
Venerable Zhi Yue 知悅法師
Zeng Jing-yi 曾靜怡
Valerie Tan

Podcast Audio Narrator 故事朗讀：
Venerable Miao Guang 妙光法師

Social Media Strategist 社群媒體策略：
Selene Chew 周思蕾

Podcast Intro & Outro Music Composer 音樂創作：
Nicholas Ng

Podcast Audio Editor 音檔剪輯：
Venerable Zhi Sheng 知笙法師

財團法人佛光山人間佛教研究院
Fo Guang Shan Institute of Humanistic Buddhism

GREYSCALE
BIN TRAVELER FORM

Cut By: Buid #21 Qty: 16 Date: 27.26

Scanned By: _____ Qty: _____ Date: _____

Scanned Batch IDs:

Notes / Exception: